Married in the Sight of God

Theology, Ethics, and Church Debates Over Homosexuality

Christian Batalden Scharen

University Press of America, ® Inc.
Lanham • New York • Oxford

4720 Boston Way
Lanham, Maryland 20706

12 Hid's Copse Rd.
Cumnor Hill, Oxford OX2 9JJ

Printed in the United States of America
British Library Cataloging in Publication Information Available

Library of Congress Cataloging-in-Publication Data

Scharen, Christian Batalden.
Married in the sight of God : theology, ethics, and church debates
over homosexuality / Christian Batalden Scharen.
p. cm.
Includes bibiographical references and index.
1. Homosexuality—Religious aspects—Evangelical Lutheran Church in America.
2. Marriage—Religious aspects—Evangelical Lutheran Church in America.
3.Sex—Religious aspects—Evangelical Lutheran Church in America.
4. Ordination of gays—Evangelical Lutheran Church in America. 5. Evangelical
Lutheran Church in America—Doctrines. I. Title
BX8074.H65 S33 2000 241'.66'088241—dc21 00—042352 CIP

ISBN 0-7618-1768-9 (cloth: alk. ppr.)
ISBN 0-7618-1769-7 (pbk: alk. ppr.)

™The paper used in this publication meets the minimum
requirements of American National Standard for Information
Sciences—Permanence of Paper for Printed Library Materials,
ANSI Z39.48—1984

To gay, lesbian, and bisexual Christians
who struggle to be faithful to their loved ones
in the midst of churches who will not yet fully welcome them,
call them to leadership,
or offer blessing on their commitments;

and to Sonja Batalden,
the one to whom I have made promises of fidelity and love

You will find many a pious priest against whom nobody has anything to say except that he is weak and has come to shame with a woman. From the bottom of their hearts both are of a mind to live together in lawful wedded love, if only they could do it with a clear conscience. But even though they both have to bear public shame, the two are certainly married in the sight of God. And I say that where they are so minded and live together, they should appeal anew to their conscience. Let the priest take and keep her as his lawful wedded wife and live honestly with her as her husband, whether the pope likes it or not, whether it be against canon or human law. The salvation of your soul is more important than the observance of tyrannical, arbitrary, and wanton laws which are not necessary to salvation.

Martin Luther,
To the Christian Nobility of the German Nation

Contents

Foreword

How do traditions confront change? *Married in the Sight of God* refuses to address the question in the abstract, but tackles it in all its messy particularity. Author Christian Scharen's attention to detail simultaneously illumines the question of change and argues that the question must be posed concretely. Concretely, then, how did the Evangelical Lutheran Church in America (ELCA), a church with roots in the Reformation of Martin Luther, come to formulate a policy which requires celibacy of its practicing homosexual candidates for rostered ministry?[1] How did this tradition confront change?

Scharen believes that practicing homosexuals otherwise qualified for positions of leadership should not be excluded from the rostered ministry of the church, but his book is no polemical brief for gay ordination or gay marriage. Churchfolk of good will on all sides of this debate will be interested in how the discussions evolved, and Scharen acts as a trustworthy pilot through the labyrinth of social statements, ecclesial pronouncements, and candidacy manuals.

This book will not be of interest to Lutherans alone. All major Protestant denominations find themselves discussing the status of same-sex marriages and homosexual ordination. In plotting the

---

1. The category "rostered ministry" included both ordained and professional church workers or AIMS, "Associates in Ministry," all of whom are listed on an official roster of candidates for ministry. They received certification through a process that Scharen describes in Chapter Four, one that involves a three stage process: pre-endorsement before entering a Masters of Divinity program, endorsement, and final approval. During the course of this process candidates move through a battery of interviews and written essays.

trajectory of debate in one communion, Scharen invites others to do the same for their own communions. In addition, he offers them the tools of his own investigation: theological insight, social analysis, and archival precision.

Finally, the scholar of religion finds in this book a provocative application of the work of Max Weber and Michel Foucault. Weber's analysis of bureaucracies and how they function illumines the candidacy process of this large Protestant denomination. Meanwhile Foucault's work uncovers the disciplinary techniques employed in the making of church leaders.

Aspects of homosexuality, either ordination or gay marriage, have topped *The Christian Century's* list of the "top ten" stories in religion for several years running. Taking the debate in one communion Scharen examines the context of the debate, offers methodological tools for its investigation, and probes theological arguments. Let me underscore each of these points.

1. Context. In the wake of the sexual revolution of the 1960s and 1970s mainstream denominations scrambled to adjust to changing cultural mores. Peacetime's cult of domesticity was short-lived: the popular post-war sit-com "Leave it to Beaver" lasted longer in the re-runs than in reality. The portrait of stay-at-home moms and slave-at-work dads shattered with the feminist movement. Women demanded equal opportunity and equal pay in the workplace. Advances in technology made contraception accessible and affordable. Divorce rose sharply across the domestic landscape. Alongside these monumental changes a gay rights movement gained ground and visibility.

Mainstream churches could not hope to escape the shifting of these cultural plates. In many the question of women's ordination rose first. Predecessor churches to the ELCA ordained the first woman pastor in 1975. But the question of rostering practicing homosexuals for ministry in the church surfaced more than ten years later, despite synodical requests for counsel in this matter dating back to the 1950s. How would the ELCA, founded only in 1988, marshall biblical and theological resources to address this question?

Official efforts to address the issue spiraled back to an appeal from the Fifties, originally deployed to encourage women to stay in the home rather than enter the workplace. Homosexuality was presented as contrary to the "heterosexual structures of God's creation." In itself this policy did not preclude homosexuals from entering rostered ministry: they had only to embrace celibacy to qualify for rostered ministry in the church, as did any other single heterosexual candidate. Heterosexual candidates, however, had the option of marriage; homosexual candidates did not.

Five hundred years ago Martin Luther fought with Rome over the issue of clerical celibacy. He regarded celibacy as a gift; the problem was that it was a gift rarely given.[2] Unfortunately, the church of his time required celibacy of those without the gift--with disastrous consequences. In contrast, Luther argued that the great majority of Christians found sexual desire to be an urge as natural and urgent as the need to eat, to drink, to eliminate. Given the enormous power of sexual desire for good and for ill, Luther commended the estate of marriage as its remedy. He wrote of marriage as an insider, treating it with a tough-minded realism and a spirit of compassion.

Five hundred years later the tradition that bears Luther's name situates itself much differently on matters sexual. Two shifts are decisive. First, moving away from Luther's earthy regard for sexual desire, latter-day Lutherans elevate sexuality from simple condition of being human to the status of "gift." Indeed, "gift" language characterizes not only Lutheran but most Protestant statements on sexuality. Certainly Luther would have agreed with the constructive potential in sexuality, but gone is his sober recognition of its equal potential for destruction. Second, because he saw sexual desire as a natural urge, Luther prescribed marriage as its remedy. Latter-day Lutherans want to be equally prescriptive, but when sexuality is the "gift," feelings of entitlement crowd in. Once entitlement enters the picture, it becomes harder to argue for constraints on the sexual activity of anyone, whether heterosexual or homosexual. How could an institution deny a group of people the opportunity to open such a gift?

2. Method. Scharen finds a consistent appeal to "heterosexual structure of God's creation" in arguments and policy limiting sexual activity to heterosexual marriage. But he stops to ask where this

---

2. The Augsburg Confession puts the matter in this way: "It is not alone God's command that urges, drives, and compels us to do this [take a wife or husband], but God's creation and order also direct all to marriage who are not endowed with the gift of virginity by a special act of God." "The Augsburg Confession," in Theodore G. Tappert (ed.), *The Book of Concord* (Philadelphia: Fortress Press, 1959), p. 74.

phrase originated and in what context. One sifts Luther's writings for it in vain. In search of the origin of "heterosexual structures of God's creation," Scharen deploys the analytical tools of Michel Foucault, particularly his notions of archaeology and genealogy. Archaeology examines the relations between text, events, and structures of power within a certain stratum of history; genealogy moves through various historical strata, to isolate a particular idea and trace its evolution. Genealogy captures different roles a concept might have played in different settings. Scharen uses both tools to illumine ecclesial arguments that appeal to language of "heterosexual structures of God's creation."

He engages genealogy to uncover the history of the concept itself. Through careful archival work and attention to the production of church social statements over the past fifty years, Scharen uncovers a fascinating story. Theologian and church executive Harold Haas coined the phrase in 1957 to protest the emerging women's movement and the disruption he feared it would create in family life. A phrase used to warn women away from the workplace in the 1950s was dusted off in the 1980s and 1990s to censure homosexuality: "heterosexual structures of God's creation."

Scharen deploys a kind of comparative archaeology of past and present to excavate the contexts in which the phrase was originally used and in which it surfaces today. His close examination of the circumstances and personalities in these two different contexts textures the argument. In the 1950s the rhetoric works to preserve male and female roles in workplace and home respectively. Homosexuality is not even mentioned under the rubric of "heterosexual structures of God's creation." In the 1980s and 1990s the rhetoric functions to exclude practicing homosexuals from the rostered ministry of the church.

Max Weber supplements Foucault in Scharen's archaeology of the present. Weber's writings on bureaucracy shed light on a candidacy process that masks the agency of the certifying institution and disciplines the candidate with procedures that encourage "correct speaking," "correct writing," and the assembly of a "correct file." Scharen leaves no doubt that detecting practicing homosexuals is the besetting concern of the process. Ironically, during this period in which the ELCA has been in heated public debate over homosexuality, an alarming amount of money has been quietly paid out to settle claims of heterosexual clergy sexual misconduct. It would seem that heterosexuality and not homosexuality is the greater problem!

3. Theological. How would all this sit with the Reformer himself? Scharen does not ignore Martin Luther's own prejudices and political accommodationism. At times Luther seemed to trade the Pope's protection for that of the princes, and his writings against the Jews and the Turks are lamentable. Yet, Scharen firmly believes that Luther could offer counsel to the present situation, if one studies him at his most radical and unconventional points.[3] He provides a reading of Luther and of the contemporary situation that exercises equally a hermeneutics of suspicion and a hermeneutics of generosity. His "middle path" proposes to listen seriously both to the voices of a tradition and to the voices of the present.

What does Scharen hear? Luther protested a tradition that devalued sex and marriage while uplifting celibacy, that made of marriage a sacramental rather than a civil affair, and that viewed the work of marriage as necessary but not properly Christian. In contrast, Luther regarded human nature, however tainted with sin, as God's handiwork. He viewed sexual desire as a genuine human need, along with the needs to eat, to sleep, to eliminate waste. Finally, Luther saw a fragility in human relationships that was matched only by the fragility of the people involved. He instructed fathers to regard the work of diapering their children as part of their Christian calling.[4] He urged the wife of an impotent husband to flee to another country and remarry.[5] And, as mentioned above, he understood that the gift of celibacy--and for Luther celibacy, not sexuality, was the "gift"--was one rarely given.

What would Luther say if he were around to argue with the church that bears his name? Undoubtedly he would be prompted to embark on

---

3. Cf. Kristen E. Kvam, "Honoring God's Handiwork: Challenges from Luther's Doctrine of Creation," in Charles P. Lutz (ed.), *A Reforming Church . . .Gift and Task: Essays from a Free Conference* (Minneapolis: Kirk House Publishing, 1995), 183.

4. Luther imagines the confession of a father and husband: "I confess to thee that I am not worthy to rock the little babe or wash its diapers, or to be trusted with the care of the child and its mother." Martin Luther, "The Estate of Marriage," in *LW* 45, 39.

5. Martin Luther, "On the Babylonian Captivity of the Church," in *LW* 36, 233-234.

a new round of spirited conversation that would have to be entitled *Pillowtalk*, not *Tabletalk*. He might argue heartily with Scharen's interpretation of context, use of tools, and theological construction. But he would certainly find in this book a worthy conversation partner--as will the reader.

Conclusion. *Married in the Sight of God* chronicles the history of debates on marriage and sexuality in general and homosexuality in particular. It also clears the ground for serious discussion of several issues which have to this point been obscured.

First, in the midst of all this talk, one has to ask what is not being discussed. Debate on the ordination of practicing homosexuals begs two prior questions. One prior question is whether or not the church could recognize committed and faithful relationship among homosexuals, as it recognizes heterosexual marriage. This question must be addressed before the issue of ordaining practicing homosexuals.

The other is more complex: what constitutes a committed and faithful relationship in the first place? The maxim "celibacy in singleness, fidelity in marriage," while crucial to the flourishing of such relationships, simply does not say enough. The high rate of divorce among Christians offers mute testimony to the insufficiency of the church's support of even the relationships it recognizes. How might the church nurture committed and faithful partnerships in its midst?

Second, Scharen's analysis of the candidacy process in the ELCA is chilling. The ecclesial bureaucracy masks its own agency in a series of impersonal and inflexible disciplinary procedures. Foucault and Weber make one doubt that anything else could be the case.

Yet every church body must take seriously the task of leadership formation, inculcating values that a person in the office will invariably need and developing competencies that their congregants will undoubtedly expect. How does a potential leader learn the appropriate exercise of his or her gifts. Let's bracket sexuality for a moment, and examine those more traditional gifts of preaching, counseling, teaching, or personal charisma? The apostle Paul tackled this ancient question in his first letter to the Corinthians (1 Cor 12). He also presented a solution: "Knowledge puffs up, but love builds up." (1 Cor 8:1) What exercise of gifts will build up the church? What is the appropriate sexual behavior of church professionals, homosexual or heterosexual, married, partnered, or single? How are they to be mentored into such conduct?

Christian Scharen's richly textured research points toward these questions. He bestows a new way of framing them, and he clears the air for the asking.

Martha Ellen Stortz
Professor of Historical Theology and Ethics
Pacific Lutheran Theological Seminary
The Graduate Theological Union

Preface

Sexuality and the Debates in Church and Society

Most major Protestant denominations in the United States agree on only one thing when it comes to relating Christianity and homosexuality--the issue causes deep conflict.[1] The United Church of Christ, a historically liberal church that ordains gay and lesbian ministers as well as blesses same-sex unions, seems to have moved beyond the fray with its appointment of William R. Johnson to a national staff position for gay and lesbian concerns.[2] Yet, most others face new developments in the struggle yearly. The Southern Baptist Convention (SBC), the nations largest Protestant body, has issued a resolution that the bible condemns homosexuality. In response to challenges, for the first time in its 177 year history, the Georgia convention of the SBC banned member churches--in both cases for allowing gay lay people to take leadership roles.[3] The United Methodist church's Judicial Council ruled in 1998 that its rules against

---

1. For a fascinating study of cross-denominational struggles on a local level, see Keith Hartman, *Congregations in Conflict: The Battle Over Homosexuality* (New Brunswick, New Jersey: Rutgers University Press, 1996), who studies Methodist, Baptist, Metropolitan Community Church, Quakers, Roman Catholics, and others in the Raleigh-Durhan area of North Carolina.

2. "UCC appoints minister to address gay issues," in *The Christian Century* 114 (April 9, 1997): 359-360.

3. "The Crucible of Kosovo: Top Religion Stories of 1999" in *The Christian Century* 117 (January 5-12, 2000): 20-21.

clergy performing same-sex unions are binding as church law. Risking their credentials in a strong challenge to this ruling, 92 United Methodist clergy participated in blessing a holy union of a lesbian couple in Sacramento, California.[4] The Presbyterian Church (USA), at its 1996 General Assembly, passed an amendment to its Book of Order requiring candidates for ordination to live in the fidelity of marriage between a man and a woman, or live in the chastity of singleness. Challenges to the so-called "fidelity and chastity" amendment have not ceased since, including elections of openly gay elders and a New York presbytery voting to allow ministers to preform same-sex unions.[5] Lutherans, Episcopalians, Catholics, and other denominations have struggled over similar issues.[6]

In response, this book suggests the need for critical studies of the particular issues and possibilities for change within each of the denominations. Without these studies, the consensus needed for change in each will be difficult to achieve. As one contribution toward this set of studies, *Married in the Sight of God* provides a case study in the contemporary debates over sexual ethics in one of the largest Protestant churches in the United States, the Evangelical Lutheran Church in America (ELCA). This study may be of use to those beyond Lutheran circles not only because of the common issues involved in the current debates but also because of the central role of Lutheranism in the origins of Protestantism. The ELCA, like other Protestant bodies, has formulated study documents on sexuality generally and homosexuality in particular. It too has heard the cacophonous voices of conservatives and liberals struggling for clarity on this difficult issue.

---

4. "Defying Church Law," in *The Christian Century* 116 (February 3-10, 1999): 105-106.

5. "Case of Gay Elder goes before PCUSA court," in *The Christian Century* 115 (January 21, 1998): 50-51; "Presbyterian body OK's same-sex unions," in *The Christian Century* 116 (February 24, 1999): 210.

6. "ELCA to maintain stance on homosexuality," in *The Christian Century* 116 (September 8-15, 1999): 843-844; "Anglicans on homosexuality," in *The Christian Century* 115 (August 12-19, 1998): 742-743; "Priest and nun barred from ministry to gays," in *The Christian Century* 116 (July 28-August 4, 1999): 738; Lisa Sowle Cahill, "Silencing of Nugent, Gramick sets a novel standard of orthodoxy," in *America 181* (August 14, 1999): 6-10.

In the ELCA, the debates center on the theological heritage of the sixteenth century Lutheran Reformation, especially the idea of marriage as an "order of creation," a fundamental relationship created by God to orient human life toward God's purposes. This idea has been at the heart of United States Lutheran theologies of sexuality over the past 60 years. These theologies were articulated in response to a variety of perceived crises in American society including "divorce," "contraception," "free-love," and "homosexuality."[7] Most recently, this theological heritage has been retrieved for use in institutional policies as a means to exclude those gay and lesbian candidates for ministry who will not commit to life-long celibacy. Challenges to the condemnation of homosexuality have come both from within and without the various Lutheran bodies during the last 30 years. In response to these challenges, Lutherans have been unable to achieve consensus on a new position, leaving them with an ultimately untenable reiteration of past arguments about marriage and homosexuality.

I argue strongly that the ELCA requires a new theological and ethical position on marriage and ordination for gay and lesbian people. Various churches have made historic shifts on key moral issues such as slavery, women's equality, divorce, and contraception. The change in deeply held moral convictions does not happen easily, nor does it happen by disregarding traditional arguments. Rather, these sorts of historic changes require critical study of the underlying theological convictions and interpretations which led to such moral judgements. Additionally, these reversals on moral judgements come after listening very seriously to contemporary voices. The critical study of Lutheran

---

7. Many difficulties accompany the question of terminology for describing those human beings who are of a sexual minority, drawn romantically to both sexes or to others of one's own sex . I recognize the very real political issues involved in naming, and thus welcome and will for the most part use the names which various gay and lesbian people and groups use to self-identify. However, as a heterosexual or straight man, I do not presume to make decisions about which terminology is "right." Therefore, on a limited basis, and with some reservation, I will use the term "homosexual" which is most commonly used by those opposed to gay and lesbian concerns. I intend to use the word in certain places, including the title of the book, exactly because this is most often the official language of the institutions to whom I refer throughout the argument.

very seriously to contemporary voices. The critical study of Lutheran theology of marriage in this work aims to play a small part in working toward a persuasive and broadly affirmed theological position that would fully bless the lives and leadership of people--gay or straight--who make life-long promises of love and fidelity, one to another.

Yet, the constructive work which would give arguments for such an affirming theological position must come second. Until work is done to show how current understandings of marriage are problematic, a constructive and affirming theological position likely will not transform the thinking of many faithful Christians. This is because the first task is to show how the normative tradition is problematic and in need of revision. Only then will the way be cleared to speak *both* faithfully from common traditions *and* with integrity in our contemporary historical moment.

My own understanding of the content and problematic nature of Lutheran theologies of marriage slowly grew through study and research, certainly. Equally important, however, was the direction, motivation, and inspiration I gained through engagement with two important aspects of my life, which will explain some of the background for this work.

The first aspect is my marriage with Sonja Batalden. The daily comforts, challenges, negotiations, and joy are the lived expression of our promises to each other. Our marriage moves me to reflect on the nature and character of marriage vows. The daily faithfulness of one person to another brings to life the promises of God, who grounds such human and frail promises. Whatever else this book may be, it certainly reflects my conviction regarding critical, committed and loving work for the up-building of marriage. Suffice it to say that my academic reflection on marriage and my lived marital commitment mutually strengthen and challenge one another.

Friendship constitutes the second aspect of my life which motivates and directs this book. Here, though, I have particular friendships in mind. These friendships with gay, lesbian, and bi-sexual Christian people transformed my understanding of God's intention for human relationship. An honest remembrance of my journey means admitting that early in my college years I argued against ordination of people of minority sexual orientation because I felt their sexuality was sinful and should not be held up as "holy living," a charge to the ordained in the Lutheran Service of Ordination. Through their gracious and loving patience, I came to know their humanity and their deep faithfulness, their pain and anguish at the rejection of the church, and their desire to befriend me. In the midst of these friendships, I struggled with scripture and with the arguments of tradition, and ultimately these experiences overwhelmed my ability and justification for condemnation. Friendship became a school in which I learned new ways of seeing, new ways of understanding, new ways of struggling together. Throughout my years in seminary, my sense of God's deep love and grace active in calling gay and lesbian friends to the ministry grew immeasurably, while at the same time, the Church's bureaucratic processes worked out ever more effective methods to exclude these friends from ordained ministry.

The first idea for the shape book came through hearing a lecture on the theology of creation with Dr. Elizabeth Bettenhausen at Re-Imagining, a conference held in November 1993 in Minneapolis celebrating the mid-point of the World Council of Churches Decade in Solidarity with Women.[8] Dr. Bettenhausen was speaking about God the weaver woman who weaves the world out of old, tired-out, good for nothing rags. She took the imagery from a poem written by Rev. Kathleen Reed entitled "Creatio Ex Nihlilo." Dr. Bettenhausen made the ethical connection between people whose clothes are ripped to shreds and the fact that my clothes are woven from those shreds. I wear them as a cloak to keep me warm. In other words, the creation of my comfortable position may *depend* on injustice toward other people. She helped me make the connection between my ease in being "heterosexual" and married and those friends of mine who, because of the gender of their partners, do not have access to the full welcome and blessing of our faith community. Thus, in a way, this book turns attention away from homosexuality and tries to portray the moral problems with the church's marriage theology. This amounts to critical inquiry into the moral status of the benefits I enjoy as a heterosexual married man.

It comes as no surprise, then, when I admit to the reader that the author's social location requires a very specific and interested perspective on the subject of this book. I am also a candidate for ordination in the Evangelical Lutheran Church in America. In no small

---

8. See Marit Trelstad and Christian Scharen-Batalden, "Remembering RE-Imagining," in *dialog* 33 (Summer 1994): 230-2.

way because I am male, white and married, I encounter few hurdles and find much encouragement throughout the process of theological and church-based formation. For example, during the "approval interview" with my candidacy committee--the required final-year examination of candidates for ordained ministry--I was asked if I would seek to fulfill the guidelines outlined in *Vision and Expectations*.[9] When I responded that I absolutely would not and that I felt the document was causing untold harm in the church, they approved me anyway with the admonition to "wait until I was ordained before speaking out on such things." The candidacy process has caused many others, some women, some international students, some of different (from me) racial and ethnic backgrounds, and certainly some of different (from me) sexual orientations, many more problems. Thus, although I had no problems in the process (and exactly because I had no problems!), I write to protest the theological and institutional rejection of gay and lesbian Christians who, rather that live a life of celibacy, wish like me to promise vows of love and fidelity to a life partner.

A note on language: I recognize that the men I quote very often use exclusive language, and I have purposefully not changed theirs. I certainly make every effort to be inclusive in my own words. However, my critical project entails showing the oppressive rationalities operative in various times and places, and how those rationalities impact the present. To change the exclusive language, an integral part of the male dominant rationalities, would be to suggest that the language is more innocent than it really is.

Although the scope of this work is narrow, and my understanding of the complex issues of our common present limited, I offer this book in humility, not knowing with certainty what God wills. Yet, my best theological reflection on these issues combined with my moral outrage at the violence and exclusion done to my brothers and sisters in the faith moves me to work for change in the church. In the words of one intellectual mentor, Michel Foucault,

> My books . . . are little tool boxes, if you will. If people are willing to open them and make use of such and such a sentence or idea, of one analysis or another, as they would a screwdriver or a monkey wrench,

---

9. Chapter four gives detailed attention to the candidacy process and the role of *Vision and Expectations* in it.

> in order to short circuit or disqualify systems of power . . . all the better.[10]

Therefore, I add this book as a tool, a screwdriver or a monkey wrench, to be used in working against the exclusion and marginalization of gay and lesbian Christians in my church. I hope others will find uses for it in their own churches, as well.

---

10. Michel Foucault in a 1975 interview in *Le Monde*, quoted in Didier Eribon, *Michel Foucault*, trans. Betsy Wing (Cambridge, Massachusetts: Harvard University Press, 1991), 237.

Acknowledgements

This book began as my masters thesis at the Graduate Theological Union (GTU) in Berkeley, California. It pains me to say that some of the people most responsible for inspiring me toward this topic can not be thanked here by name for it would compromise their status as ministers in the church. Still, to those gay and lesbian friends, my deepest thanks for your friendship and support, then and now.

Various professors at the GTU, at Pacific Lutheran Theological Seminary, and at the University of California, Berkeley challenged and directed my thinking on this project at various stages: Don Compier; Barry Stenger; John Coleman; Karen Lebacqz; Michael Aune; Walter Stuhr; Donna Duensing; Timothy Lull; Robert Bellah; Paul Rabinow. I especially own a debt to friends who met for two years reading Luther under the direction of Reformation Historian Dr. Robert Goeser: Aana Vigen and Kelly Denton-Borhaug. Each have continued to encourage me on this project in various ways.

My thesis advisor, mentor, and friend, Martha Ellen Stortz, offered all sorts of help and direction, from start to finish, including reading the entire manuscript at numerous stages. She has exemplified scholarly collegiality for me; whatever is good about the book I owe in part to here positive influence.

DeAne Lagerquist, one of my original thesis committee members and Professor of Religion at St. Olaf College, graciously shared her vast knowledge of Lutheranism in the United States. Her friendship and support over the years helped to push this project along.

Since moving to Emory University in Atlanta where most of the revisions have been done, I benefitted from other influences, and incurred more debts. To my teachers here, some who have helped directly and all who have encouraged and supported me, thank you:

Elizabeth Bounds; Nancy Eiesland; James Gustafson, John Gunneman; Timothy Jackson; Don Saliers; Steven Tipton; Theodore Weber.

When I had a contract for the book, I invited a cadre of my fellow doctoral students to come over for an Italian feast in exchange for a critical reading of the manuscript as a whole. Their critical commentary made the book much better than it was; had I been able to heed all their advice, the book would be much better still. Yet, I am deeply grateful for the enthusiasm they showed for the book; thanks to Susan Hylen, Robert Jones, Ted Smith; Bradley Schmeling; and Melissa Snarr.

Charles Lutz, former head of the Office of Church and Society for the American Lutheran Church, helped along the revisions by generously reading and responding to the whole manuscript. I admire his decades of church leadership; as a lay Lutheran, he has worked within and through the ALC and now the ELCA to challenge the church to live out its faith in the world on behalf of the poor and oppressed. His support and encouragement means very much.

My parents, Albert and Vicki Scharen, read and responded to a final draft, offering the most valuable of gifts: proofreading. Their support has been great. As well, my in-laws, LaVonne and Paul Batalden, have supported and encouraged me in addition to faciliting time away from an active toddler in order to finish rewriting.

A version of chapter 4 was previously published in "Subject to Discipline: Authority, Sexuality, and the Production of Candidates for the Ordained Ministry," in *Journal of the American Academy of Religion* 68 (Summer 1998):89-120.

Lastly, I owe most to Sonja and Isaiah who together teach me daily about marriage, family, love and commitment. Without the "reality check" they provide, drawing me away from the computer to make breakfast, read a story, or go for walk to the park, I might be tempted to think a book is more important than it truly is.

C.B.S.

Atlanta, Georgia
Lent 2000

Chapter 1

The Times Have Changed: Reflections on Doing Christian Sexual Ethics Today

> "The stupid canon lawyers want to apply laws that were framed in other times and for other reasons. They say, 'Thus it is written in the book,' and they don't see that the times have changed and that former circumstances and laws have passed away."
>
> Martin Luther
>
> "Marriage Laws Must be Adapted to the Times" (1539)

Martin Luther's typically bold remarks about canon lawyers and marriage laws set the agenda, if not the tone, for this chapter. This book is largely about contemporary parallels of Luther's complaint--that is, about marriage theology and church laws based upon it that no longer fit the times. Luther arrived at this strong conviction through his hard won theological insights, but also, and just as importantly, through the experiences forged in his pastoral work with struggling men and women. In order to make the argument that the church suffers from a similar set of circumstances today, and thus needs new theology and church laws regarding sexuality, I offer the reader a chance to reflect with me in advance about how to make such an argument.

In part, this is an issue of an author's integrity in relation to you, the reader. If I ask the reader to see ways that the current theology of marriage in the church and the church policies that embody it are problematic, the reader deserves to know the method of critique leading to such a conclusion. Further, if I go on to say that parts of traditional theological positions should be let go and others rehabilitated for contemporary use, the reader deserves to see the method of constructive argument leading to such judgements.

This chapter briefly presents the method used in the book. Some readers, following Jeffery Stout, may feel that "preoccupation with method is like clearing your throat: it can only go on so long before you lose your audience."[1] If so, they may wish to move quickly to the end of the chapter where I outline the arguments of chapters two through five. For other readers, the following sections will deepen their understanding of my approach in the book as a whole. I hope that they will actively question both the coherence of the method as well as the fruitfulness of its impact on the unfolding critical, historical, and constructive work to follow. Such methodological reflection is both important for my clarity and central for the reader in understanding why certain resources are used in particular ways to serve the overall arguments.

Method: Critical Christian Ethics

Work on sexual ethics, and especially homosexuality, very often focuses on the morality of individual acts, and the validity of personal beliefs backing up such judgements about moral and immoral acts.[2] Indeed, traditional approaches in ethics center on understanding aspects of individual action in an effort to say what is right for one to do in certain circumstances. To some degree, this is right and good. The moral life is finally lived out by people who must decide how to act.

---

1. Commenting on academic theology in his book *Ethics After Babel: The Language of Morals and Their Discontents* (Boston: Beacon Press, 1988):163.

2. A recent example that deals in a very clear manner with many related issues but fundamentally turns on the morality of same-sex acts is Stanley J. Grenz, *Welcoming but not Affirming: An Evangelical Response to Homosexuality* (Louisville: Westminster/John Knox, 1998). Mark Jordan's fine historical treatment of *The Invention of Sodomy in Christian Theology* (Chicago: University of Chicago, 1997) shows that the term sodomy came about because of the need to label and also judge sexual acts of all sorts outside of the procreative intercourse between a married man and woman.

Yet, such a focus biases Christian ethics in such a way that one no longer clearly sees the Christian community as the context for moral life.[3] The danger here is that if Christian ethics were only about the individual and what he or she desired, moral life would run the risk of becoming what Robert Bellah and his colleagues have termed "Shelism." This religion of one could be described as a social and spiritual withdrawal into one's own world where one pursues "self-fulfillment" toward idiosyncratic ends.[4] In this view, deeply rooted in the ideology of the 'rugged individual' who must make it alone, lies a trap which can draw Christians into self-saving and defensive actions. One example, also taken from Bellah and his colleagues, is the phenomenon of gate and wall enclosed "life-style enclaves" which now represent the majority of suburban landscapes.[5] Without a critical Christian community within which to live out a moral life, one is at the mercy of the mores of the dominant culture of individualism and self-aggrandizement.

Living out a moral life in a Christian manner may never mean simply "fulfilling myself" or moving to a relatively encased, homogenous place in which I feel safe. The Christian life is not, despite popular opinion, doing what "seems right to me." Not that one's human experience is excluded from the process of decision making. On the contrary, it is central. But the question of individualism and the moral life raises a consideration of the utmost importance for ethical reflection: as Lutheran ethicist Larry Rasmussen argues, humans "are essentially and not accidentally community moral beings. The self is fundamentally communal."[6] Christian ethics has

---

3. Stanley Hauerwas has argued these themes most strongly. See, among his many works, *The Peaceable Kingdom: A Primer in Christian Ethics* (Notre Dame: University of Notre Dame Press, 1983).

4. Robert N. Bellah, Richard Madsen, William M. Sullivan, Ann Swidler, and Steven M. Tipton, *Habits of the Heart: Individualism and Commitment in American Life* (Berkeley: University of California Press, 1985), 235ff.

5. Bellah, et. al., *Habits of the Heart,* 71 ff; Edward J. Blakely and Mary Gail Snyder, *Fortress America: Gated Communities in the United States.* Palo Alto: Brookings Institution, 1996.

6. Larry Rasmussen, *Moral Fragments and Moral Community: A Proposal for Church in Society* (Minneapolis: Fortress Press, 1993), 125.

an irreducibly relational, communal shape.[7] The resulting communal or relational self works, in the United States, to de-center a mythic self--reliant individual who values autonomy and individual rights, and who constitutes self-hood over against another person. In contrast to the myth of the 'rugged individual,' a communal self comes into being through the stories of the parents, community, and society in which that self grows.

For a Christian community, then, the senses of God and the stories of the faith which shape identity inform and deform the way in which that community or a person from that community might respond to any given situation. The action following would have consequences directly related to the community's sense of God, and the stories of faith told in that place. What consequences unfold from certain combinations of community understanding of the good and stories of faith? How do these understandings and stories shape the assumed norms by which a community interprets its sources and thereby decides to act in certain ways?

Such questions about the structure of a community's life and its joint actions form the direction of the Christian ethical analysis in the work which follows. James M. Gustafson has put it very well in describing H. Richard Niebuhr's work:

> Ethics helps us to understand ourselves as responsible beings, our world as the place in which the responsible existence of the human community is exercised. Its practical utility is in its clarification, its interpretation, its provision of a pattern of meaning and understanding in the light of which human action can be more responsible.[8]

Therefore, in order to achieve this clarifying and self-critical role, Christian ethics benefits from adopting a set of critical theoretical tools used to analyze how character is shaped, how norms come to be, how norms influence moral rules, and the consequences of actions based upon these norms and rules.

---

7. One might also turn to H. Richard Niebuhr's *The Responsible Self: An Essay in Christian Moral Philosophy* (New York: Harper & Row, 1963) for another strong argument for the fundamental relational and communal nature of moral life.

8. James M. Gustafson, "Introduction," in Niebuhr, *The Responsible Self*, 18.

The critique of what is being thought, said, and done need not end with criticism, however. The critique "does not merely consist in saying, 'I protest,' but in making of that attitude a political phenomenon that is as substantial as possible, and one which those who govern, here or there, will sooner or later be obliged to take into account."[9] Ethical critique opens up new possibilities for life together.

Critical Tools: Archaeology and Genealogy

This brief discussion sets out the analytical tools which undergird the term "critical" in my method of critical Christian ethics. The approach follows Michel Foucault, especially in his deployment of a set of analytical tools--archaeology and genealogy--which may be used diagnostically on the present. That is, Foucault offers a way of doing critical history in order to "show how particular domains of knowledge have constrained human freedom and to provide the intellectual resources for overcoming these constraints."[10] Foucault's analytical tools allow me to show the various contexts in which the "orders of creation" theology became dominant in 20th century Lutheran studies on sexual ethics. Then, his approach gives me a way to show the *use* of this dominant theology in the formation of ELCA policies aimed at excluding gay and lesbian people from ordained church leadership. Genealogy serves further serves the argument of the book through locating alternative theological positions present in the church's tradition but prevented from rehabilitation by the power of the dominant view currently enforced by official church policy.

Foucault encouraged the sort of focused and critical work this book embodies; he liked work groups and constantly aimed his research toward the goal of informing ongoing political issues.[11] His work

---

9. Michel Foucault, "Politics and Ethics: An Interview," interview by Paul Rabinow, Charles Taylor, Martin Jay, Richard Rorty, and Leo Lowenthal (Berkeley, April 1983), *The Foucault Reader*, ed. Paul Rabinow (New York: Pantheon Books, 1984), 377.

10. Gary Gutting, *Michael Foucault's Archaeology of Scientific Reason* (Cambridge: Cambridge University Press, 1989), 2.

11. See Keith Gandal, Stephen Kotkin, and Paul Rabinow, eds., *History of the Present: A Newsletter*, (February 1985). *History of the Present* was published for a few years after Foucault's death in 1984 by the Graduate Division at the University of California, Berkeley as a forum for

aimed at rather specific, humble ends. Rather than resisting all domination, explaining the root of violence in humanity, or overturning all contemporary culture, he aimed to:

> give some assistance in wearing away certain self-evidences and commonplaces about madness, normality, illness, crime and punishment; to bring it about, together with many others, that certain phrases can no longer be spoken so lightly, certain acts no longer, or at least no longer so unhesitatingly, performed; to contribute to changing certain things in people's ways of perceiving and doing things; to participate in this difficult displacement of forms of sensibility and thresholds of tolerance--I hardly feel capable of attempting much more than that.[12]

Foucault used the terms "archaeology" and "genealogy " to describe the tools by which to accomplish this wearing away of certain self-evidences.[13]

Foucault's views arose out of the mid-century debates over the legacy of phenomenology, especially the efforts of hermeneutics and structuralism, to overcome the Kantian subject/object division upon which phenomenology depends. Although his efforts at the study of human beings differed from those three options, they each influenced his development, language, and therefore the academic traditions with which he is now often associated. Whereas structuralism looks for a

conversation between the various work groups either organized by Foucault himself or inspired by his work.

12. Michel Foucault, "Questions of Method," trans. Colin Gordon in *The Foucault Effect: Studies in Governmentality*, eds. Graham Burchell, Colin Gordon, and Peter Miller (Chicago: The University of Chicago Press, 1991), 83.

13. Various efforts to split Foucault's work into chronological periods of his life obscure more than they illumine. It may be valuable to speak of the emphasis in his methods of working as shifting. According to one reliable account, "There is no pre- and post-archaeology or genealogy in Foucault. However, the weighing and conception of these approaches changed during the development of his work." See Hubert L. Dreyfus and Paul Rabinow, *Michel Foucault: Beyond Structuralism and Hermeneutics*, 2nd ed. (Chicago: University of Chicago Press, 1983), xxv. Gilles Deleuze, a colleague of Foucault, sees a third methodological component present in the later 1980s work on subjectivity and sexuality. Deleuze terms this "subjectivation." See Gilles Deleuze, *Foucault,* trans. and ed. Sean Hand (Minneapolis: University of Minnesota Press, 1986), 94ff.

deep logic which constitutes the universal structure of social life, Foucault's early books are read correctly as an attempt to work out a different path, an archaeology, as he put it, which tries "to define the relations on the very surface of discourse; I attempt to make visible what is invisible only because it's too much on the surface of things."[14] Foucault attempted to show, by describing the "rules" governing the articulation of serious discourse in the human sciences, how these "rules" also govern the production of statements. After the publication of *The Archaeology of Knowledge*, his first and only purely methodological work, he rethought his approach in order to focus less on the project of a theory of rule-governed systems of discursive practices. Rather, he shifted emphasis in order to have archaeology serve a new approach derived from his reading of Friedrich Nietzsche: genealogy.

As Hubert Dreyfus and Paul Rabinow show, "from his earliest days Foucault used variants of a strict analysis of discourse (archaeology) and paid a more general attention to that which conditions, limits, and institutionalizes discursive formations (genealogy)."[15] Beginning in the early 1970s and leading into the brilliant work, *Discipline and Punish* (1976), Foucault uses archaeology as a technique. Again, Dreyfus and Rabinow: "As a method of isolating discourse, [archaeology] serves to distance and defamiliarize the serious discourse of the human sciences. This, in turn, enables Foucault to raise the genealogical questions: How are these discourses used? What role do they play in society?"[16] Foucault explained his theoretical adoption of genealogy as a way to map the occurrence of ideas, not "in order to trace the gradual curve of their evolution, but to isolate the different scenes where they engaged in different roles."[17] In other words, he turned "away from the attempt to develop a theory of discourse, and uses Nietzsche's genealogy as a starting point for developing a method

---

14. Michel Foucault, "The Archaeology of Knowledge" in *Foucault Live* (Interviews, 1966-84) trans. John Johnston and ed. Sylvère Lotringer (Columbia University, New York: Semiotext(e) Foreign Agents Series, 1989), 46.

15. Dreyfus and Rabinow, *Michel Foucault: Beyond Structuralism and Hermeneutics*, xxv

16. Ibid.

17. Michel Foucault, "Nietzsche, Genealogy, History," in *The Foucault Reader*, 77.

that would allow him to thematize the relationship between truth, theory, and values and the social institutions and practices in which they emerge."[18]

This method of inquiry "requires patience and a knowledge of details, and it depends on a vast accumulation of source material."[19] The genealogist must suffer the

> affliction of those enamored of libraries, documents, reference works, dusty tomes, texts that are never read, books that are no sooner printed than they are consigned to the shelves of libraries where they thereafter lie dormant . . .[20]

In these dusty tomes, the genealogist begins work, digging, sifting, searching for the gaps and lost arguments which the winners of the struggles have systematized or glossed over. These subjugated knowledges present in the written history help relativize and historicize what the present moment has crowned natural or a given or, as Lutheran theologian William Lazareth states, "unchangeably normative."

Genealogy unites the critical work of the archivist with these contested positions which were buried or left behind in the shifting trajectory of history so that the reigning knowledges can be challenged by the subjugated positions long forgotten. Foucault writes,

> a genealogy should be seen as a kind of attempt to emancipate historical knowledges from that subjection, to render them, that is, capable of opposition and of struggle against the coercion of a theoretical, unitary, formal, and scientific discourse. It is based on a reactivation of local knowledges . . .[21]

---

18. Dreyfus and Rabinow, *Michel Foucault*, xxv.

19. Ibid., 77-8.

20. Michel Foucault, "Two Lectures," in *Power/Knowledge: Selected Interviews and Other Writings, 1972-1977*, ed. Colin Gordon and trans. Colin Gordon, Leo Marshall, John Mepham, and Kate Soper (New York: Pantheon Books, 1980), 79.

21. Ibid., 85.

Such genealogical work, therefore, asks first about those points of view that were left behind and how these forgotten positions can serve a alternatives to today's main ideas.

From this methodological position, I join Foucault in proposing to do the history of the present. A history of the present focuses not on simple interest in the past, but in understanding the layers of the present through a close analysis of the past.[22] Oftentimes, this style of research shows that certain rules and obligations exist written in civil code or the moral discourse of the Church which "claim to temper and prevent violence that would supposedly exist without their civilizing restraints. But the genealogist protests, these noble expressions are the very means by which domination advances."[23] In short, the burden of my critique lies in showing that while the ELCA portrays its theology of marriage and related policies as embodying God's intention for human relationships, in fact the ELCA quickly adopted this theology in an effort to ensure institutional stability, doing unjustifiable harm to many persons in the process.

Constructive Use of a Tradition

Anger at unjustifiable church policies and their harmful effects motivated Luther and motivates me in the work of constructive Christian ethics.[24] In response to Luther's remarks about canon lawyers and marriage laws at the beginning of the chapter, I suggested that this chapter should not only relate my method of critique, but also my method of construction. If my critique persuades some readers that parts of the tradition should be left aside, how might the constructive argument find resources in the church's traditions to recover for contemporary use? The challenge, as historian Mark Jordan has put it,

---

22. Michel Foucault, *Discipline and Punish: The Birth of the Prison*, trans. Alan Sheridan (New York: Vintage Books, 1979), 30-31.

23. Dreyfus and Rabinow, *Michel Foucault: Beyond Structuralism and Hermeneutics*, 216.

24. While anger cannot always lead to the most rational and clear-headed thinking, it can at times be motivated by moral outrage that serves in the work of love toward God and one's neighbor. See Beverly Wildung Harrison, "The Power of Anger in the Work of Love," in *Making the Connections: Essays in Feminist Social Ethics*, ed. Carol S. Robb (Boston: Beacon Press, 1985), 3-21.

is to "honor the tradition while being faithful to the Gospel and to the impulses of God in the present."[25]

Using the Varieties of Sources

Listing the four main sources for a systematic Christian theological ethics up front foreshadows my discussion regarding which sources I will attend to and why. Here I follow the work of James M. Gustafson, a leading Christian ethicist, who suggests that a major task of systematic theological ethics consists of judgements about the validity and relevance of the materials used as content for the ethical proposal. Gustafson claims that

> a comprehensive and coherent Christian theological ethics must be adequate with reference to the following sources : (a) the historically identifiable sources of Christian thought, that is, the Bible and the Christian tradition; (b) philosophical methods, insights, and principles; (c) scientific information and methods that are relevant and about which there is little dispute; and (d) human experience broadly conceived, including the consequences of the theological ethics when applied to human action.[26]

These sources are as much descriptive as normative; most ethicists include each whether explicitly or implicitly.

Gustafson, however, does not recommend ad hoc and implicit usage of sources. Rather, he emphasizes the fact that all Christians have a perspective that determines the judgements to be made and these should be made explicitly. He suggests judgements must be made "about (a) which sources are valid and relevant; (b) which sources are to be

---

25. Jordan's discussion of "the responsible construction of Christian moral tradition" very helpful. He remarks that in order to make a change on some significant moral issue, believers "first had to free themselves from fundamental misunderstandings about the character of Christian moral tradition. Part of freedom is to remember how fragile our relationship to that tradition is, so far as it is a relation dependant on the reading of inherited texts." See *The Invention of Sodomy in Christian Theology*, 170-176.

26. James M. Gustafson, *Protestant and Roman Catholic Ethics: Prospects for Rapprochement* (Chicago: University of Chicago Press, 1978), 142.

decisive when they conflict and why; (c) what specific 'content' is to be taken and what is to be ignored from these sources, and why; and (d) how this 'content' is to be interpreted and why it is interpreted as it is."[27] Such judgements are of central importance because what one determines to be the primary source will have significant effects on the use of the other sources.

Theology as well as science, Gustafson notes, regularly presumes that new research begins by a close examination of the tradition of reflection on a specific issue. Theologians have, on the whole, a greater reverence for the received traditions than their counterparts in the sciences and thus often attend to certain Scriptural texts or figures in the Christian tradition with devoted and sometimes uncritical care. Nonetheless, both theology and science develop in response to new historical circumstances, new methodological or technological tools, and new insights into God and the world. In theology new views develop, Gustafson argues, "in part by abandoning aspects of what is received including what is received in the charter document, the Bible."[28] One can give examples of this sort of change: decisive new views have been developed on issues such as slavery, religious liberty, and the equality between men and women.[29] For Lutherans, one could add the marriage of clergy and the ordination of women.

Given the reality that changes in prescriptive ethics often entail the abandonment of aspects of the received tradition, I will examine the question of change and prescriptive sexual ethics with some care. Raising terms such as the abandonment of certain scriptural or other traditional resources surely raises the eyebrows of many faithful Christians. And well it should; it is serious and often painful business when the community tries to discern what God is doing here and now and how it should respond. Nonetheless, it is simply a fact that interpretation and choice must accompany the interpretation and usage of Scripture and tradition, as well as the use of philosophy, science, and

---

27. Gustafson, *Protestant and Roman Catholic Ethics*, 142.

28. James M. Gustafson, *Ethics from a Theocentric Perspective, Vol. I: Theology and Ethics* (Chicago: University of Chicago Press, 1981), 144. This section is Gustafson's book is a rich and challenging reflection on the use of tradition in constructive theological work.

29. Gregory Baum, "Homosexuality and the Natural Law," *The Ecumenist* (January-February 1994): 35.

experience. While many will want to say that Scripture is divinely inspired, few wish to completely deny its fundamental historical character and thus be required to follow such chilling directives as stoning to death rebellious children in Deuteronomy 21: 18-21. Similarly, many wish to hold Luther's work in the highest esteem but few would affirm his encouragement of the slaughter of the peasants in 1525 or his diatribes against the Jews late in his life.

In working out a way to affirm a new ethic for marriage and sexuality, I wish to find a middle path, a path that avoids some clearly immoral prescriptions within scripture and tradition but that also avoids a similarly untenable concession to the whims of contemporary society. I argue that this middle path requires attention to human experience, including what is known through the sciences as well as everyday life, held in tension with the witness of Scripture and tradition. An explication of this view serves my constructive comments in chapter 5 where I show that in fact this view represents not only how Luther worked when making a change in his time, but how Lutherans have worked when they made their most serious effort to bring the resources of tradition to bear on what God is doing in the present day. These methodological views lead to a focus on certain theological groundings from the tradition, groundings which will be fundamental to any revision of ethical relational theology.

Revision in Sexual Ethics

Seen from a practical standpoint, James Gustafson argues, sexual morality exists in order to give shape to biological drives in ways that limit harmful actions and encourage beneficial ones.[30] While in some societies and in some historical eras, moral strictures regarding sex remain tacit, the last two generations in most western developed nations experienced rapid and radical changes in the formerly tacit sexual moralities. Among the challenges were the advent of mass-marketed contraceptive drugs, a relaxing of social and religious condemnation of divorce, changes in gender roles, the emergence of gay and lesbian communities, the legalization of abortion, and cohabitation.

---

30. In the following paragraphs I depend on James M. Gustafson, "Nature, Sin, and Covenant: Three Bases for Sexual Ethics" *Perspectives in Biology and Medicine* (Spring 1981): 483ff.

Challenges from society make contemporary Christians painfully aware of how out of step traditional Christian regulations regarding sex appear; indeed, the strictness of Christian sexual morality has also come under great attack from Christians themselves as profoundly anti-human, anti-body, and anti-woman.[31]

That is, Christian sexual morality has come under attack in places where it is contrary to human experience. Today many find a goodness in sexuality; it provides a place where one can experience some of life's most profound pleasures and delights. These pleasures can of course refer to the physical responsiveness of one to another and yet it also includes the wonder of learning about the intricacies of bodies as God has created them, the mutuality and trust that can accompany such physical intimacy, and certainly for some the process of bearing and raising children. A caution: simple statistical "normality" of a certain sexual ideal or practice does not constitute a valid warrant for change in moral rules. For example, while masturbation is "normal" and now seen by many as one aspect of healthy psycho-sexual growth, one could argue that violence against women is also statistically "normal" yet it is decidedly unhealthy for the victim, for the perpetrator, and for society at large. Still, statistical "normalcy" can in some cases be an indication of a gap between human experience and ethical prescriptions. When moral rules are deemed quite contrary to human nature and experience, they are ignored by many. Thus, at least on a descriptive level, human experience provides a key test for the continuing validity of ethical prescriptions.

James Gustafson argues persuasively, however, that there are certain bases in human experience which echo the deepest insights of the Christian tradition as it has dealt with the issues of sexuality and

---

31. This point is a staple component of progressive sexual ethics over the last thirty years. See the influential statement by James B. Nelson, *Embodiment: An Approach to Sexuality and Christian Theology* (Minneapolis: Augsburg, 1978), 19ff; A recent work that consciously builds and extends Nelson's work is Marvin M. Ellison, *Erotic Justice: A Liberating Ethic of Sexuality* (Louisville: Westminster/John Knox 1996). Yet even more conservative theologians such as Max Stackhouse argue that "forms of dualism adopted by some Christians have been anti-sensual." See his recent *Covenant and Commitments: Faith, Family, and Economic Life* (Louisville: Westminster/John Knox, 1997), 34.

marriage. It is these insights which underlie current prescriptive ethics and it is these insights which must be recovered if revisions in prescriptive ethics are to honor traditional sources while aiming to speak to the needs of the current historical moment. These three bases of human sexual experience are the following.

> First, sexuality is part of our biological and personal natures. About the first there can be no dispute; by personal, I mean to suggest that our sexuality relates to our sense of identity, of human worth and fulfillment, and so forth. Second, our experience of sin, of human moral fault, is deeply related to our sexuality. . . . Third, sexuality is related to our experience as social beings, and particularly to our need for covenants.[32]

These three experiential bases provide a descriptive lens on the wisdom of traditional Christian ethics as well as some insight about how and why arguments for change in prescriptive ethics met with some success in certain circumstances.[33]

Gustafson offers some elaboration on each of the three bases: nature, sin, and covenants. Emphasis on procreation in Christian sexual ethics required primary emphasis on the biological, reproductive aspect of human nature; yet this was never completely successful for it did not do justice to the personal nature of humans. Revisions of the procreative prescription have centered on this argument. Yet these revisions, sometimes in the name of "sexual liberation," left aside the second basis: sin. Tacit trust necessarily goes along with sexual expression and intimacy which leads to some sort of bond or commitment, an insight at least as old as St Paul (1 Cor. 6:12-16). Using another for careless pursuits of self-fulfillment is only one of the many forms that sexual exploitation can take. Thus, revisions in Christian sexual ethics

---

32. Gustafson, "Three Bases for Sexual Ethics," 487.

32. Experience can be a slippery term. Margaret A. Farley, reflecting on the role of experience as a source for ethics, uses this fine definition: "the actual living of event s and relationships, along with the sensations, feelings, images, emotions, insights, and understandings that are part of this lived reality." Her wonderfully thoughtful essay is "The Role of Experience in Moral Discernment," 134-151 in Lisa Sowle Cahill and James F. Childress, eds., *Christian Ethics: Problems and Prospects* (Cleveland: The Pilgrim Press, 1996).

need to attend to the power of the human propensity to sin. The difficulties of human sin raise the third basis, covenants, that are aimed at fostering an environment in which trust and confidence can flourish. Surely, such explicit commitments to one another serve a traditional purpose as "dikes against sin" but just as surely they may express and reinforce fidelity and mutual love. These three bases--nature, sin, and covenant--offer a grounding for entertaining changes in prescriptive ethics so that, while some resources from Scripture and tradition are necessarily left aside, fundamental insights are drawn on nonetheless.

An Outline of the Book

This book traces the events behind the present debates over sexuality in the Evangelical Lutheran Church in America. Chapter two examines one layer of the contemporary debates by offering an interpretation of Martin Luther's views on marriage. This section describes Luther's break with the view of marriage as a sacrament and his reformulation of a view of marriage as a civic affair, shared by Christian and non-Christian alike. Yet, he held the work of marriage as one of the Christian's highest callings, "a school of character" (Bainton) in which a Christian learns faith active in love toward the nearest of neighbors, one's marriage partner. Although Luther did not address the same questions being addressed today, *use* of Luther's views seems a necessary qualification for the present conversation in the ELCA. That Luther's words will be used today is a given. However, because Luther spoke to a very different set of historical circumstances, the critical question to be raised as the argument moves ahead is *how* Luther is used, and with which *effects.*

Chapter three examines a second layer of the current debates with a focus on how Luther is used in Lutheran theologies of marriage published by the predecessor bodies of the ELCA, beginning with the revival of United States Lutheran social ethics in the late 1940s and early 1950s. I offer an archaeology of a particular interpretation of marriage as an "order of creation" that is now talked about as "normative" in ELCA documents and by many bishops and theologians. The contemporary root of this interpretation of marriage, commonly expressed as "the heterosexual structure of creation," stems from a 1957 article by theologian and church executive Harold Haas.

This expression circulates in the present conversations, albeit to ends quite different from those originally invoked by Haas. While Haas employed the phrase both to reify traditional gender roles against the feminist movement for equality and to protect the sacredness of sexual expression in an age when contraceptives became widely available, Lutheran ethicist Robert Benne was recently quoted invoking Haas' language of the "heterosexual structure of the order of creation" as justification for promoting marriage, while at the very same time and on the same exact theological basis marginalizing gays and lesbians.[34]

Chapter four turns to genealogical questions, to questions of the institutional use of the "order of creation" theology and its effects on persons. I will examine how this theology of marriage provided the basis for the ELCA's response to a crisis over the ordination of "openly gay" seminarians in Berkeley just as the ELCA came into being. The process of certifying candidates for ordained ministry clearly developed in certain ways in order to control the clergy population, especially in ways to keep gay and lesbian candidates either celibate or out of the (preparation for) ministry.

Chapter five reflects on the ways in which the ELCA and its predecessors have interpreted their tradition and which choices they have made about selecting from that tradition in order to deal with the circumstances of the day. I will not argue with the fact of selectivity; it is a given that some resources will be drawn upon and others left aside. Therefore, making a move to open up new possibilities, I suggest that the Evangelical Lutheran Church in America has powerful resources in its own traditions with which to reorient its present trajectory. Through an interpretive strategy of looking for the ways human experience leads to the unconventional arguments, I point to possible resources in Luther's work as well as in the work of previous Lutheran statements on marriage and sexuality. These include: a strong claim that humans are only rarely given the ability for celibate life, a bold affirmation of nature and embodiment, recognition of the sexual drive itself as a blessing from God, and an affirmation of the covenantal character of marriage relationship which mirrors the faithfulness and self-giving love of God toward the world. While responding to several potential challenges, I nonetheless show these

---

34. *San Francisco Chronicle* cover story (11/29/94), "Americans Search for New Sexual Ethic." See chapter three below.

resources are sufficient to fashion a sexual ethic that fully welcomes gay and lesbian Christians while also upholding key essentials of the church's historic position on marriage--a position both faithful to the tradition and to the contemporary moment.

In the conclusion, I reflect on theology and social change. I raise questions about the ability of critical historical and theological-ethical work to change minds and hearts without personal experiences in relation to gay and lesbian Christians. As an example of such a personal and transformational experience, I relate the story of ELCA bishop Paul Egertson. With his spouse, Shirley, Egertson struggled to respond to the news that his oldest son is gay. The Egertson's journey of understanding leads them from condemnation and denial to acceptance and celebration.

Chapter 2

Honoring God's Handiwork: Luther on Sexuality And Marriage

When Lutherans argue over the church's proper stance toward current social issues, whether sexuality or any other topic, they turn to see what Martin Luther had to say. Luther's work is the touchstone for a church that, in the words of Timothy Lull, depends on theology as "the glue that has most often held us together through these last five centuries."[1] While Anglicans might worry over liturgical precedent and Catholics may rehearse a tradition of Papal pronouncements, Lutherans turn to theological claims to adjudicate disputes and inevitably turn first to Luther. Therefore in order to move the argument of the book forward into the debates of the present I must venture an interpretation of Luther's views on sexuality and marriage despite the dangers of doing so without the credentials of a reformation historian. I trust that what I show in the following chapter represents an accurate and judicious reporting of some of the findings of various reformation historians as well as my considered views.

As the reader would expect, I present Luther in ways I consider both fair to the historical record and helpful to my developing argument. This should not invalidate my interpretation but rather require of me, as it should of any interpreter, arguments showing why I wish to draw on Luther in the ways that I do--this task I will take up more formally in chapter five. This chapter begins by arguing that Luther's creative theological work in the area of sexuality derived its motivation and aim

1. Timothy F. Lull, "The (Normative) Sexual Hole," *dialog* 32 (Winter 1993): 66.

from his pastoral experience. He took the stories of troubled parishioners, fellow priests, and nuns to his study of Scripture and tradition, working out a perspective that centers on justification as participation in Christ, by faith, as alone sufficient for salvation.[2]

In the following two sections, I then unfold Luther's understanding of the effect of participation in Christ. A first section of the chapter outlines the two major revisions in the (Western[3]) Church's view of sexuality and marriage wrought by Luther -- in conjunction with others -- on the basis of his mature theology. The shifts were, first, the critique of a two-tiered Christianity that outlined one way for the spiritual elite and another less holy way for the laity. Luther toppled this system of merit-based pursuit of salvation; he "horizontalized Christian ethics."[4] The second shift was from a sacramental understanding of marriage, under the governance of the church, to a notion of marriage as an civil estate common to all humans. These shifts document Luther's overall effort to relocate the God-pleasing arena of Christian action from the cloister, pilgrimages, etc. (a self-serving system based on personal accumulation of merit) to the home, the work-place, and the neighborhood (an other-serving system based on the forgiveness of God freeing the faithful Christian to love those in need). The relocation of the arena of Christian action will undergird the description of the two shifts.

The second section sketches Luther's mature views on marriage. Luther's mature views reveal both difficulties--such as the idealization of marriage as the proper destiny of all people[5] and some strikingly

---

2. Carl E. Braaten and Robert W. Jenson , eds. *Union with Christ: The New Finnish Interpretation of Luther*, (Grand Rapids: Eerdmans, 1998), esp. 1-41.

3. The Church catholic had already split into East and West, in part on the issue of the celibacy of clergy. See Luther's comment in "To The Christian Nobility," 176.

4. Heiko Oberman, *Luther: Man Between God and The Devil*, trans. Eileen Walliser-Schwarzbart (New York: Doubleday, 1989), 80. He wrote, "Luther horizontalized Christian ethics: he transferred its goal from Heaven to earth. Good works are not required for salvation but crucial for surviving in a threatened world."

5. Luther always held out that some might be able to remain celibate, but recognized with St. Paul (1 Cor. 7: 7) that "such persons are rare, not one in a thousand, for they are a special miracle of God." Cf. Luther, "Estate

unconventional views, i.e., where he did not follow traditional positions. These points where Luther departed from the dominant views of his day--such as the claim that humans are rarely given the ability for celibate life, that sexuality is created good even if marred by sin, and that marriage is fundamentally about promise making and fidelity, our's and God's, and that attention to pastoral experience is central to theology--are the most important for my argument.

The Primacy of Pastoral Concerns

In 1512, Martin Luther began duties in Wittenberg as Professor of Bible at the University and in 1515 as parish priest at the Castle Church. Under the careful guidance of the vicar of the Augustinian order, Johann von Staupitz, Luther slowly began moving toward his revolutionary recovery of the radical gospel of God's grace in Jesus Christ.[6] Once found, Luther's grasp of this "one glowing core, namely, the gospel of the forgiveness of sins,"[7] did not shift throughout the rest of his career. Luther continued to work out the consequences of this core vis á vis the realities of contemporary Catholicism which he knew intimately. According to one biographer, "Luther probed every resource of contemporary Catholicism for

---

of Marriage," 21.

6. For Luther's own description of this discovery, See "Description of Luther's 'Tower Experience' (1532)," trans. and ed. Theodore G. Tappert, *LW 54*, 193.

7. Einar Billing, *Our Calling,* trans. Conrad Bergendoff (Philadelphia: Fortress, 1964) 4. Cf. George Forell, *Faith Active in Love: An Investigation of the Principles Underlying Luther's Social Ethics* (Minneapolis: Augsburg, 1954), 64. Forell's book, still one of the finest interpretations of Luther's views on the Christian life, argues that this "central importance of the relationship of God to man as established by the gospel of forgiveness of sins is the key to Luther's method (64)." "As far as Luther is concerned, all ethics is based upon God's forgiveness of sins (63)." Although I do not have space here to work out this theological or evangelical basis upon which Luther made his social and political comments, I happily refer the reader to Forell as well as to William Lazareth, *Luther on the Christian Home: An Application of the Social Ethics of the Reformation* (Philadelphia: Muhlenberg, 1960) and to the important new Finnish research on Luther's view of justification by faith in *Union with Christ,* Braaten and Jenson, eds.

assuaging the anguish of a spirit alienated from God."[8] This experience of searching anguish led Luther to pay keen attention to the spiritual well-being of his parishioners, as well as fellow priests, monks and nuns.

Luther's pastoral concern for the burdened consciences of his flock related directly to what he understood to be unconscionable abuses of ecclesiastical authority. Luther's protector and prince, Frederick the Wise, the elector of Saxony, had fallen deeply into the system of indulgence sales--Frederick's collection of relics in the Castle Church "illustrated by Lucas Cranach in 1509 listed 5,005 particles, to which were attached indulgences calculated to reduce purgatory by 1,443 years."[9] The crown of the collection was an authentic thorn from Christ's crown, which was reputed to have actually pierced the Savior's forehead. Theologian and Luther scholar Timothy Lull wrote that the

> selling of indulgences developed slowly throughout the Middle Ages. Originally its conception was limited to removing the temporal or earthly punishments that the church had the right to inflict as part of the sacrament of penance. But it was clear to Luther that many simple persons were not understanding indulgences in this way. Those who arranged for their sale had their own stake in keeping the precise theology of indulgences obscure.[10]

It is against this system and on behalf of his flock who were being led astray that Luther wrote what may be his most famous work, "The Ninety-Five Theses" or, according to its official title, "Disputation on the Power and Efficacy of Indulgences."[11] This proposal for academic

---

8. Roland H. Bainton, *Here I Stand: A Life of Martin Luther* (New York: Mentor Books, 1950), 40.

9. Ibid., 53.

10. Timothy F. Lull, "Introduction to Part I: The Task of Theology," in *Martin Luther's Basic Theological Writings*, ed. Timothy F. Lull (Minneapolis: Fortress, 1989), 9.

11. Thus he wrote: "51. Christians are to be taught that if the pope knew the exactions of the indulgence preachers, he would rather that the basilica of St. Peter were burned to ashes than built up with the skin, flesh, and bones of his sheep." Martin Luther, "The Ninety-Five Theses (1517)," in Ibid., 26.

debate, written in Latin and directed to Luther's colleagues, became a touch-stone of lay protest against the clerical abuses of Rome.[12]

Up to 1520 Luther's growing anger at the abuses of Rome had basically remained matters of the University and Castle Church in Wittenberg. His German works "were pastoral works for laymen, advising them what to do and expect in the confessional, in prayer, as god-parents at a christening, at mass, and not least when in mortal danger."[13] His Latin works, however, full of specific rebuttals and detailed biblical exposition, were "aimed at a specialized audience, for colleagues a chance to change, for students a chance to learn."[14] Finally the burden of responsibility became too great; his conviction-driven, trembling words written in early 1520 set the stage for his growing public stature and influence: "So farewell, ill-fated, doomed, blasphemous Rome! The Wrath of God has come upon you . . . ."[15] In his first foray into the public realm, Luther wrote a passionate, pastoral, and quite successful political tract, *Address to the Christian Nobility of the German Nation*. As priest and professor, Luther spoke out to the German princes on behalf of their subjects, his flock, who were "oppressed by distress and affliction" and were made to "cry out time and time again and to pray for help."[16]

---

12. After years of frustrated effort at evangelical reform, Elizabeth, duchess of Brunswick/Lüneberg, issued her own reform mandate in 1541. The effect of Luther and the other reformers on her view, especially on indulgences, is clear in the following:

> Have we not in the past been shamefully led astray from the Gospel and the truth by human commandments and teaching? What did we know about catechism, that is, the moral and religious training of children, before the Gospel reappeared? What did we know about the correct celebration of the Eucharist? When did anyone teach us correctly about the forgiveness of sins, justification, truly good works, and the holy cross? Did not the clergy go about preaching pure fables? Had it not reached the point that forgiveness of sins was being sold for money in a remarkable insult to the merit of Christ? If any would deny this, let him tell us why the indulgence has been so wide spread in Germany?

Steven Ozment, *Protestants: The Birth of a Revolution* (New York: Doubleday, 1992), 98.

13. Oberman, *Luther: Man Between God and The Devil*, 41.

14. Ibid., 42.

15. Ibid., 43.

16. Martin Luther, "To The Christian Nobility of the German Nation

As an example of this distress and affliction, Luther discusses the sad state of the priesthood. Many priests' consciences were troubled because they had wives and children, yet church officials did nothing to help them. Luther felt help *could* come easily if someone would just speak the truth. Taking this task upon himself, Luther wrote: "I will redeem my conscience and open my mouth freely, whether it vexes the pope, bishop, or anybody else."[17] He began quoting I Timothy 3:2, 4 and Titus 1:6-7 to make the case that a priest should not be compelled to live celibate and alone, but should be permitted to have a wife. Luther's pattern of argument in defense of the goodness of sexuality and marriage for all, clear already here and later developed to a sharp edge, consists of taking seriously scriptural witness and bodily experience over against the dictates of canon law and the papacy. He concluded, on the basis of 1 Timothy 4:1, 3 ("There shall come teachers who bring the devil's teaching and forbid marriage."[18]), that the Roman regulation against clerical marriage was wickedness--"so much misery has arisen from this that tongue could never tell it."[19]

Luther's advice, based on the Christian liberty of the priests, was that they may marry in order to avoid the temptations so prevalent. Luther shared a deep discouragement with other reformers over the widespread nature of these problems.[20] He was sure that because God has not commanded and bound priests to celibacy, no priest should regard such a vow as valid, nor should anyone offer such a vow to remain celibate. Here Luther intends to leave the decision whether or not to marry open to the civic order and to an individual's good judgement.

This openness to the civic order's right to control marriage law foreshadows Luther's decisive rejection of marriage as a sacrament a few months later in his treatise, "The Babylonian Captivity of the Church."[21] Despite his concern to leave this decision open, he felt the

Concerning the Reform of the Christian Estate (1520)," trans. Charles M. Jacobs and revised James Atkinson, *LW 44*, 124.

17. Ibid., 175.

18. Throughout this chapter, I use Scripture texts exactly as Luther has them in his text.

19. Luther, "To The Christian Nobility," 176.

20. For a discussion of these concerns among Luther and his fellow reformers, see Steven Ozment, *The Age of Reform 1250-1550: An Intellectual and Religious History of Late Medieval and Reformation Europe* (New Haven: Yale University Press, 1980), 383ff.

21. Cf. "Shifts Toward the Neighbor " below for the shift from marriage

need to offer comfort to "that pitiful band who with wives and children have fallen into disgrace and whose consciences are burdened because people call them priest's whores and their children priest's children. As court-jester I say this openly."[22] The comfort offered by Luther eloquently unfolds his position:

> You will find many a pious priest against whom nobody has anything to say except that he is weak and has come to shame with a woman. From the bottom of their hearts both are of a mind to live together in lawful wedded love, if only they could do it with a clear conscience. But even though they both have to bear public shame, the two are certainly married in the sight of God. And I say that where they are so minded and live together, they should appeal anew to their conscience. Let the priest take and keep her as his lawful wedded wife and live honestly with her as her husband, whether the pope likes it or not, whether it be against canon or human law. The salvation of your soul is more important than the observance of tyrannical, arbitrary, and wanton laws which are not necessary to salvation.[23]

Truly, this brilliant and angry tract to the Christian Nobility (and to the public who read the treatise[24]), reflects the clear insight of a theologian, but even more clearly, a pastor's moral outrage at the burdens laid on the consciences of the people.[25]

Luther did not make his audacious suggestions on the basis of institutional authority, but rather out of his growing understanding of the Christian's authority and responsibility "to advise and help my

---

as sacrament to marriage as civil estate.

22. Luther, "To The Christian Nobility," 177.

23. Ibid.

24. Heiko Oberman writes that although the tract "was ninety-six pages long, four thousand copies were printed and virtually torn out of the hands of the Wittenberg publisher Melchior Lotter. Only a few days later a second edition had to be printed in Wittenberg, and editions of the tract were soon published in Leipzig, Strasbourg, and Basel." Oberman, *Luther: Man Between God and The Devil*, 41. Also, see Mark U. Edwards, Jr. *Printing, Propaganda, and Martin Luther* (Berkeley: University of California Press, 1994).

25. Dr. Robert Goeser, Professor of Historical Theology at Pacific Lutheran Theological Seminary and the Graduate Theological Union in a seminar on Luther's social thought, Spring, 1994.

neighbor. . . ."[26] On this authority he makes three points which aim to break the highest institutional authority, the Pope, and his opinion on the question of clerical marriage. First, he argues against the common practice of allowing a priest to pay fines (called "*Hurenzinss*") to the local bishop in order to have a woman living with him, but disallowing marriage. He likened this practice to "putting straw and fire together and forbidding them to smoke or burn!"[27] Second, God created in humans a desire for one another. Luther argues that "the pope has as little power to command this as he has to forbid eating, drinking, the natural movement of the bowels, or growing fat."[28] Luther laments the many consciences which are confused and tortured as a result of the requirement of clerical celibacy. Third, Luther lifts the command of Christ, that what God joins together no one shall put asunder, above the vast and complex regulations of canon law which forbid marriage on the basis of a multitude of so-called "impediments."[29] Luther pronounced his judgement that in "the entire canon law of the pope there are not even two lines which could instruct a devout Christian, and, unfortunately, there are so many mistaken and dangerous laws that nothing would be better than to make a bonfire of it."[30] He concluded that the marriage of clergy was no offense before God or the Holy Scriptures. Further, any Christian could declare dispensation from the laws of the Church, for Christ has set us free from all human laws, "especially when they are opposed to God and the salvation of souls, as St. Paul teaches in Galatians 5:1 and I Corinthians 10: 23."[31] Nervous princes and hopeful priests must have gone straight to their Bibles after reading the conclusion to this section of Luther's treatise.

For those who want a clear formulaic statement, Luther was a frustratingly pastoral figure. He did not often write systematic texts for the hallowed halls of the academic world, and even those writings are full of concern for the plight of burdened priests, nuns, and the many

---

26. Luther, "To The Christian Nobility," 178.

27. Ibid.

28. Luther, "To The Christian Nobility," 178.

29. Cf. the discussion of Steven Ozment, *When Fathers Ruled: Family Life in Reformation Europe* (Cambridge, Massachusetts: Harvard University Press, 1983), 44-49.

30. Luther, "To The Christian Nobility," 178.

31. Ibid., 179.

confused "simple Christians" who did not understand the Latin of the liturgy or the original Greek and Hebrew of the scriptures. Luther felt these servants of the church deserved respect and careful teaching on the part of those called to be their leaders. As a result, his writings are topical and chock-full of scripture. Luther did not make rules where evangelical freedom could be allowed to decide what may be best. For example, in advising clerics on the struggle to be chaste, he clearly states God's creation of sexuality as a natural urge and ordinance of marriage as God's intention. On this basis, they should avoid vows of celibacy. Yet, he writes:

> Some have indicated even more things to be avoided, e.g. soft beds and clothes, excessive adornment, the company of the opposite sex, speaking to them or even looking at them, and whatever else in the same vein that is conducive to chastity. In all these things no one can fix a definite rule or limit. Every man must find out what is conducive to chastity in his case.[32]

Luther clearly moved from his theological insights into the realm of Christian life with profound pastoral realism and a keen sense for evangelical freedom.

Luther's views on sexuality and marriage have usually been characterized with the terminology of "social ethics" or "dogmatics." Exactly because of the primacy of his pastoral concern for burdened consciences, modern day interpreters do an injustice to Luther if they mine his work for applicable principles for today's troubles. Luther did not do this himself! Rather, through study of scripture, application of reason, and prayer, all held in view of his pastoral experiences, he applied his deeply held theological insights to the lives of those whom he encountered along the way. As one Reformation scholar has said, "Luther used precise, but not technical language."[33] Ethics, so-called, might for Luther be described as practiced faith, or better, as Luther himself explained it: "Surely we are named after Christ [Christians] because we believe in him and are *Christs one to another* and do to our

---

32. Martin Luther, "Treatise on Good Works (1520)," trans. W.A. Lambert and revised James Atkinson, *LW 44*, 105.

33. Dr. Robert Goeser, Professor of Historical Theology at the Pacific Lutheran Theological Seminary and the Graduate Theological Union in a seminar on Luther's social thought, Spring, 1995.

neighbors as Christ does to us" (italics mine).[34] When we see "in the Spirit" our eyes are changed so that we see Christ in our neighbor, and whereas our faith serves God, all our love flows to the needs of our neighbors.[35]

Luther's Revisions in Moral Teaching

From a Two-Tiered Ethic to a Horizontal Ethic

The scholastic ethics of Luther's time found its distinctive grounding in a merit-based system of salvation which claimed that "Christian ethics was not the road of life in fellowship with God, but rather the road leading to fellowship with God."[36] Luther found in the church of the High Middle Ages an extremely complicated system of gradations of sins and various capabilities of monks, clergy and laity in the fulfillment of the works necessary to salvation. Ordinary Christians were not thought to be able to fulfill the "highest" works of poverty and chastity, through which great suffering and therefore holiness and merit were gained. These "holy" works created a treasury of merits, which by purchase of an indulgence and acts of confession and penance could help lift the sinful laity to the higher plane of holiness and closer fellowship with God. The following, an autobiographical moment in Luther's "Lectures on Genesis," shows the hierarchy of holiness:

> When I was a boy, the wicked and impure practice of celibacy had made marriage so disreputable that I believed I could not even think about the life of married people without sinning. Everybody was fully persuaded that anyone who intended to lead a holy life acceptable to God could not get married but had to live

---

34. Martin Luther, "The Freedom of a Christian (1520)," trans. W. A. Lambert and revised Harold J. Grimm, *LW 31*, 368.

35. Commenting on Galatians 5:6, Luther writes, "As I have said, therefore, Paul is describing the whole of the Christian life in this passage: inwardly it is faith toward God, and outwardly it is love or works toward one's neighbor." See "Lectures on Galatians 5-6 (1535)," trans. Jaroslav Pelikan, *LW 27*, 30.

36. Forell, *Faith Active in Love*, 73.

as a celibate and take the vow of celibacy.[37]

Luther's critique of this two-tiered Christianity[38] comes to full clarity and power in his 1520 work, "Treatise on Good Works." By looking closely at his argument in this text, which might best be described as a commentary on the Ten Commandments of Moses, the contours of his critique may be drawn out with some clarity. First, however, helpful perspective is gained in a brief look at an earlier treatment of the Ten Commandments. Luther's "A Brief Explanation of the Ten Commandments, The Creed, and The Lord's Prayer" was published in 1520, but was written as a series of sermons in 1517, just before he wrote the "Ninety-Five Theses." This text gives a sense of the classic medieval form in the treatment of these issues, as well as the ways in which Luther's evangelical theology began to affect his treatment of Christian life.

This "*kurz* " or "brief" form was an ancient and common catechetical tool primarily drawing upon the Creed and the Lord's Prayer.[39] Given its original use by priests for the instruction of Christians, the addition of the Ten Commandments to the other two components understandably became more common in the late Middle Ages as a result of a growing focus on the sacrament of penance. The typical use of the Ten Commandments was the classification of sins, first by the priest who heard confession, and later, after the invention of the printing press, by the laity as they prepared for confessional. As was the practice, after listing a summary of the Ten Commandments, Luther first listed transgressions against each and then works in

37. Martin Luther, "Lectures on Genesis 1-5 (1535-1545)," trans. George V. Schick, *LW 1*, 135.

38. The most important modern interpretation of this medieval merit-based ethical system and Luther's intervention shifting it towards an ordinary, common, but at the same time, very rigorous view of the "good works" of Christian life was worked out by Karl Holl in 1919 under the title, "Der Neubau der Sittlichkeit." A translation of this text from the German, with some editing, is available as: Karl Holl, *The Reconstruction of Morality*, ed. James Luther Adams and Walter F. Bense and trans. Fred W. Meuser and Walter R. Wietzke (Minneapolis: Augsburg, 1979), esp. 32-80.

39. Here I am relying on Charles M. Jacobs, "Introduction to 'A Brief Explanation'," in the *Works of Martin Luther, The Philadelphia Edition, Vol. 2* (Philadelphia: Muhlenberg, 1943), 351-353. Hereafter, *PE*.

fulfillment of each. These sermons foreshadow Luther's mature positions on the Christian's responsibility to God and to the world.

A first suggestion of an "evangelical simplicity"[40] in Luther's understanding of what must be done or not done comes at the end of all the listing of transgressions against the commandments. Luther had been brief in comparison to the typical pattern of listing all possible sins in a hierarchy of their resultant seriousness, followed by the penance required. He concludes the transgression section with: "From all this it follows that the commandments command nothing but love and forbid nothing but love; nothing but love fulfills the commandments and nothing but love breaks them."[41] Then, after a listing of the proper fulfillment of each of the commandments, Luther gives, in capsule form, the argument underlying the shift away from the medieval two-tiered ethic. He wrote:

> Thus you see that the Ten Commandments contain, in a very brief and orderly manner, all the teaching that is needful for man's life; and if a man desires to keep them, he has good works for every hour of his life, and has no need to choose him other works, to run hither and thither, and do what is not commanded.[42]

Luther's later work on the Ten Commandments is nothing else than drawing out the consequences of this powerful and compact statement.

The full implications of Luther's shift came to a mature exposition in his later "Treatise On Good Works." The occasion for this treatise was increasing criticism that Luthe's stress on justification by faith alone led to lawlessness and immorality. This concern was particularly expressed by the princes; mindful of this concern, Luther dedicated the treatise to John, the brother of Elector Frederick, Luther's sovereign. Even in such a royal introduction, Luther emphasizes that his validation in writing comes in no small part from the pastoral effects on troubled lay people:

---

40. Lazareth, *Luther on the Christian Home*, 139.

41. Martin Luther, "A Brief Explanation of the Ten Commandments, The Creed, and The Lord's Prayer (1520)," trans. Charles M. Jacobs, *PE* 2, 364.

42. Ibid., 367.

> Although I know full well and hear every day that many people think little of me and say that I only write little pamphlets and sermons in German for the uneducated laity, I do not let that stop me. Would to God that in my life time I had, to my fullest ability, helped one layman to be better! I would be quite satisfied, thank God, quite willing then to let all my little books perish.[43]

By closely looking at his argument in this text, Luther's clear pastoral concern shines forth in and through his critique of the two-tiered ethical system.

Luther opens by stating that there are no good works except those commanded by God; when the young rich man asked Jesus what he might do to inherit eternal life (Matt. 19:16-22), Jesus points him to the Ten Commandments. First among these, clearly, is the good work of faith in Christ. It is "in this work that all good works exist, and from faith these works receive a borrowed goodness."[44] Luther asks if any of those who accuse him of abolishing works would view a person's daily tasks which nourish the body and build up the community as good works. He assures the reader that indeed they would not, for "they define good works so narrowly that they are made to consist only of praying in church, fasting and almsgiving."[45] Luther retorts that God is served by anything done in faith, whether thought, spoken or done, according to Romans 14: 23 ("Whatsoever is not done of faith or in faith is sin"). With faith, God gives the spirit and with it love, peace, joy and hope.

On this foundation, then, Luther pulls the rug out on any hierarchy of "good" works. In faith, all works are equal: all distinctions disappear in the sight of God. This is because they are not accepted for what they are but on the basis of faith. Therefore, as "Samuel said to Saul, 'You shall become another man when the spirit enters you; do whatever your hands find to do, for God is with you' [I Sam. 10- 6-7]."[46] Luther is making an effort here to unpack the consequences of his view of evangelical freedom. Those who ignore this commandment to place confidence, trust, and faith in God alone "want to make God favorably disposed to them and want to buy God's grace directly from him with

43. Luther, "Treatise on Good Works," 22.
44. Ibid., 24.
45. Ibid.
46. Ibid., 26.

their many good works (as they call them), as if God were a huckster or a journeyman who did not want to grant his grace and favor for nothing."[47] By showing that no one can be righteous before God, Luther can claim that it is only by the mercy and grace of God that any works can be called good. "Faith, therefore, does not originate in works; neither do works create faith, but faith must spring up and flow from the blood and wounds and death of Christ."[48]

As Luther continues through the commandments, he returns again and again to the ground of grace-created faith, the only basis for doing truly good works in love. But he goes further by his focusing on the simplicity involved in obeying the commandments and, therefore, pleasing God. Luther writes, explaining the work of the second commandment ("You shall not take the name of God in vain"):

> The wonderful and righteous judgement of God is based on this, that at times in the privacy of his home a poor man, in whom nobody can see many great works, joyfully praises God when he fares well or with entire confidence calls upon him when he is in adversity. He does a greater and more acceptable work by this than another who fasts and prays much, endows churches, makes pilgrimages and burdens himself with great deeds in this place and that.[49]

Luther claims that what counts as a great deed will usually be marked by the small show it makes and the insignificance with which it is regarded.

In a particularly instructive section, Luther defends the Christian's responsibility for defending and speaking the "truth"--which he considers to be God's name and honor itself. Many serve themselves through defending the powerful, the wealthy, and of course, their friends. Luther bemoans the general regard for the great and powerful works and peoples of the world at the expense of basic and important work of defending the poor:

> Look, there are plenty of good works to be done! Most of the mighty, most of the rich, and most of their friends are unjust and

---

47. Ibid., 31.
48. Ibid., 38.
49. Ibid., 41.

> exercise their power over the poor, the lowly, and over their opponents. The more powerful they are, the worse their deeds. And where one cannot prevent this by force and help the truth, one can at least confess the truth and do something for it by our words, not the kind which please the unrighteous or agree with them, but those which speak the truth boldly.[50]

When Luther considered why God would not do this directly, since God is able and knows how to help all who need it, he replies that God wants our help. God "does us the honor of wanting to effect his work with us and through us."[51] As Karl Holl put it, "whoever has really become one with God in faith is thereby drawn into, indeed plunged into, the activity of God himself. One becomes an instrument, a link, a channel through which God lets his blessings flow to others."[52]

Luther applies this powerful perspective in his exposition of the Fourth Commandment ("You shall honor your father and mother"). Here he draws upon Christ's imagery from Matt. 25:35-36 in encouraging parents to see the work of caring for their children as most precious works when done in faith and confidence that God is well-pleased. Luther lays out with passion his critique of the two-tiered system in this beautiful description of marriage and family (still five years before he himself married):

> Just think what a great lesson this is! How many good works you have at hand in your own home with your own child who needs all such things as these like a hungry, thirsty, naked, poor, imprisoned, sick soul! O what a blessed marriage and home that would be with such parents! That home would indeed be a true church, a chosen cloister, yes, a paradise![53]

He rhetorically asks where such parents are, who will inquire about good works such as these. They are not grand, glittering works, Luther replies, and therefore the flesh and the devil pull you away from these works. There is no pomp or show about them; therefore, we assume they are worth nothing. Husbands run to St. James, wives make vows

---

50. Ibid., 51.
51. Ibid., 52.
52. Holl, *The Reconstruction of Morality*, 85.
53. Luther, "Treatise on Good Works," 52.

to Our Lady. Parents do not vow to train and teach themselves and their children to honor God properly.[54]

In this juxtaposition, on the one hand, of faith-inspired action according to God's creative will for the world, and, on the other, of self-concerned action according what is impressive in worldly terms, Luther's full view of the nature of Christian life was worked out for the first time. From this basic stance, Luther argues for a new view of sexuality and marriage beginning in the next two treatises he wrote, "To the Christian Nobility of the German Nation" and "The Babylonian Captivity of the Church," both written within six months of the completion of his "Treatise on Good Works." It is to the "Babylonian Captivity of the Church" that I now turn in order to examine the second of the two major shifts, the move from a sacramental understanding of marriage to a civil understanding.

From Marriage as Sacrament to Marriage as Estate

At the outset of Luther's section on marriage in "The Babylonian Captivity," he reviews the core definition of sacrament by which he has judged the other so-called seven sacraments.[55] According to Luther, "in every sacrament there is word of divine promise, to be believed by whoever receives the sign, . . . the sign alone cannot be a sacrament."[56] Since Scripture cannot justify either of these two criteria, marriage cannot be a sacrament. Additionally, the ancients, as well as the unbelievers in Luther's day, held marriage in high esteem. Given that some of the "Christian" married folk were more wicked than the unbelievers, how could marriage be a sacrament for Christians and not

---

54. Ibid., 86.

55. Some months before the writing of this book, Luther wrote to his friend George Spalatin that "there is no sacrament except where there is a direct divine promise, exercising faith. We can have no intercourse with God except by the Word of him promising, and by faith of man receiving. At another time you shall hear more about their fables of the seven sacraments." See *Luther's Correspondence and Other Contemporary Letters,* vol. 1, eds. and trans. Preserved Smith and Charles Jacobs (Philadelphia: Lutheran Publication Society, 1913), No. 206.

56. Martin Luther, "The Babylonian Captivity of the Church (1520)," trans. A.T.W. Steinhäuser and revised Frederick C. Ahrens and Abdel Ross Wentz, *LW* 36, 92.

for others? For Luther, this would be as silly as the (also common) argument that temporal power only belonged to the church.

Luther goes on directly to address the exegesis of the defense of marriage as a sacrament. The argument was made on the basis of Ephesians 5: 31-32, which according to the Latin translation in the Vulgate read, "The two shall become one. This is a great sacrament." First, Luther remarks that the word "sacrament" is nowhere used in the sense of sacrament such as the Lord's Supper or baptism. Luther chides the scriptural savvy of the papal theologians: "This argument like so many others betrays great shallowness and a careless and thoughtless reading of Scripture."[57] Rather, he goes on to show, the Greek word *mysterion* would be better translated "mystery." Luther concludes that "they have transformed the Scriptures according to their own dreams, making anything out of any passage whatsoever."[58]

However, Luther does not stop with a rather quick debunking of marriage as a sacrament; he goes on to criticize the ways in which "this divinely ordained way of life has been ensnared"[59] in the various regulations in canon law. Because this treatise is written in Latin and was sure to be read by many priests, Luther takes on the most common book used for confession, the *Summa de Casibus Conscientiae*, which treated alphabetically all possible cases of trouble for Christian conscience. Eighteen impediments to marriage were listed under the heading, "Matrimony", which Luther deals with by category. Luther recognizes how complex this area of canon law had become. He laments that if he "enters into details, the treatise will grow beyond all bounds. Everything is in such dire confusion that one does not know where to begin, how far to go, and where to leave off."[60] Nevertheless, Luther's argument turns present-day jurisprudence on its head. He laid out his view on law and civil affairs:

> This I do know, that no state is governed successfully by means of laws. If the ruler is wise, he will govern better by a natural sense of justice than by laws. If he is not wise, he will foster nothing but evil through legislation, since he will not know what use to make of the laws, nor how to adapt them to the case at hand.

---

57. Ibid., 93.
58. Ibid., 94.
59. Ibid., 96.
60. Ibid., 97-98.

> Therefore, in civil affairs more stress should be laid on putting good and wise men in office than on making laws; for such men will themselves be the very best of laws, and will judge every variety of case with a lively sense of equity. And if there is knowledge of the divine law combined with natural wisdom, then written laws will be superfluous and harmful. Above all, love needs no laws whatever.[61]

Luther argued that canon law's condemnation of marriage fails on both important points. Canon law neither follows a natural sense of justice nor the dictates of divine law.[62] On these grounds, he removes the foundation of the Church's control over marriage.

The two shifts sketched out above may become more clear as the discussion now moves to a careful outline of Luther's full view of marriage. Chronological treatments of Luther's development on these issues exist,[63] so this next section attempts to lay out the coordinates of his work by attention to three interrelated topics: marriage as God's ordinance, as a civil estate and the ground of all political authority, and, finally, as a Christian calling where the neighbor can be served in faith-activated love.

A Sketch of Luther's Full Views on Marriage

According to Reformation scholar Steven Ozment, the ideals of marriage and fidelity had fallen into crisis in Luther's time. He writes

---

61. Ibid., 98. On Luther's use of the term "equity," which he took from the Greek *epikeia*, in relation to law, see H. G. Haile, "Algorithm and *Epikeia*: Martin Luther's Experience with the Law," *Soundings* 61 (Winter 1978): 508.

62. John Witte, Jr. argues that the evangelical jurists did, however, draw heavily on canon law in formulating their own judgements on matters of marriage and divorce. See Witte's fine *From Sacrament to Contract: Marriage, Religion, and Law in the Western Tradition* (Louisville: Westminster/John Knox, 1997), 42-73.

63. The best, as noted above, is Lazareth, *Luther on the Christian Home*, esp. chapters five and six in which he argues that Luther arrived at his mature views on marriage by late 1523, more than a year before his own marriage. Therefore, as has been noted by Oberman, as well, Luther married in order to put flesh onto his pastoral and theological convictions, and to spite the devil.

that "concubinage and sexual promiscuity were wide-spread in the later Middle Ages; still in the sixteenth century an estimated one-third to one half of urban populations were unmarried adults (one-third in the countryside)."[64] Martin Luther worried a great deal about this and wrote on numerous occasions in an effort to counter popular negative views. On one occasion, he emphasized that "what we would speak of most is the fact that the estate of marriage has universally fallen into such awful disrepute. There are many pagan books which treat of nothing but the depravity of womankind and the unhappiness of the estate of marriage, such that some have thought that even if Wisdom itself were a woman one should not marry."[65] He continues:

> So they conclude that woman is a necessary evil, and that no household can be without such an evil. These are the words of blind heathen, who are ignorant of the fact that man and woman are God's creation. They blaspheme his work, as if man and woman just came into being spontaneously! I imagine that if women were to write books they would say exactly the same thing about men.[66]

Luther's plucky response here foretells his first answer to those who would deny marriage which God has created and intended as a blessing.

Yet, I take some caution in my heralding of Luther's progressive views on women and marriage. Luther was still a living out of the belief that women were inferior to and should be obedient before men, not on account of God's intention in the original creation, but as a result of sin. Thus, at least on one occasion, Luther stated that "Whenever Katie gets saucy, she gets nothing but a box on the ear."[67] Even if this was not the overall tenor of their relationship, still it is

---

64. Ozment, *When Father's Ruled*, 41-2.

65. Martin Luther, "The Estate of Marriage,"36.

66. Luther, "The Estate of Marriage," 36. Also, see Paul R. Hinlicky, "Luther against the Contempt of Women," *Lutheran Quarterly* 2 (Winter 1988): 515-530.

67. Preserved Smith, *The Life and Letters of Martin Luther* (Boston: Houghton Mifflin, 1911), 180. Cf. Luther, "Lectures on Genesis 1-5", 68-69, *LW* 1; Joy M. K. Bussert, *Battered Women: From a Theology of Suffering to an Ethic of Empowerment* (New York: Lutheran Church in America, 1986).

very troubling. One must always hold Luther's negative side in tension with Luther's positive work on behalf of the position of women in society.

Sexuality and Marriage as Divine Ordinances

Luther held a bifocal view on sex itself. Although Luther often spoke of sex as a natural bodily function, like eating, drinking and movements of the bowels, he also clearly believed that sex constituted God's divine ordinance which functions to draw humans into relationship; the "act which attracts sex to sex is a divine ordinance."[68] Luther built his defense of this view by turning to the accounts of creation in Genesis.

Luther grasped a basic truth in his reading of Genesis 1:27 ("So God created man . . . male and female he created them") and Genesis 1:31 ("He himself called it a good creation.") : each one of us must be what God has created us. We can be no other. Luther continued by boldly proclaiming a view quite contrary to popular opinion:

> Moreover, [God] wills to have his excellent handiwork honored as his divine creation, and not despised. The man is not to despise or scoff at the woman or her body, nor the woman the

---

68. Martin Luther, "Examples of the Faulty Proofs of the Papists (1538)," *LW 54,* 324. It should be noted here that Luther held very negative views about same-sex relationships. In fact, he only mentions homosexuality a few times in his writings; he was aware of its presence, but he simply did not often mention it. Luther did not interpret Romans 1: 26 as referring to homosexuality. In his Genesis lectures, referring to the story of Sodom, Luther uses the opportunity to polemicize the Monks and Rome. He writes, "Moses proceeds with a description of a terrible sin. I for my part do not like dealing with this passage, because so far the ears of the Germans are innocent of and uncontaminated by this monstrous depravity; for even though this disgrace, like other sins, has crept in through an ungodly soldier and a lewd merchant, still the rest of the people are unaware of what is being done in secret. The Carthusian monks deserve to be hated because they were the first to bring this terrible pollution into Germany from the monasteries of Italy. Of course, they were trained and educated in such a praise-worthy manner at Rome." See Luther, "Lectures on Genesis 15-20 (1535-1545)," trans. George V. Schick, *LW* 3, 251-2.

> man. But each should honor the other's image and body as a divine and good creation that is well-pleasing unto God . . . .[69]

The living Word, found through struggle with scripture, spoke to Luther with more authority than even the early church fathers.[70]

Moving along in Genesis, Luther takes God's blessing and saying to the two humans, "be fruitful and multiply" (Genesis 1:28) as sure evidence that man and woman must come together; it is beyond human control, a natural and necessary thing. Luther put it this way:

> [the injunction to be fruitful and multiply] is more than a command, namely, a divine ordinance which it is not our prerogative to hinder or ignore. Rather, it is just as necessary as the fact that I am a man, and more necessary than sleeping and waking, eating and drinking, and emptying the bowels and bladder. It is a nature and disposition just as innate as the organs involved in it.[71]

God's Word has created humans with this natural sexual urge toward another. We can not make it otherwise; "flesh and blood remain flesh and blood, and the natural inclinations and stimulations have their way without let or hinderance, as everyone's observation and experience testify."[72]

---

69. Luther, "The Estate of Marriage," 17-18.

70. In an important and rarely quoted passage from Luther's commentary on Gen. 1:27 in his "Lectures on Genesis 1-5," 61, he commented on the wildly allegorical interpretations of the fathers as to the meaning of the image of God. He wrote that the "very dangerous opinions of the fathers were discussed in all the churches and schools, but I really do not see what the fathers intended to achieve by them. Therefore my advice is to read them with discretion. They often speak as a result of an emotion and of a particular mood which we do not have and cannot have, since we do not have similar situations." The church today could learn from this evangelical freedom in terms of which interpretations of Scripture are authoritative!

71. Luther, "The Estate of Marriage," 18.

72. Martin Luther, "The Large Catechism," in *The Book of Concord: The Confessions of the Evangelical Lutheran Church*, trans. and eds. Theodore G. Tappert, et. al. (Philadelphia: Fortress Press, 1959), 393-4. Hereafter, cited as BC.

Marriage, then, was seen as a divinely ordained way to live out this sexual instinct which God's Word has created in all humans. Luther scholar and biographer Heiko Oberman gets this point exactly: for Luther, "God's power is not confined to marriage; it is already present in the sexual instinct. Marriage is simply the right way to use it, the genuinely spiritual, divinely ordained status to live one's sexuality."[73] Luther often uses this argument in letters or comments to priests, monks and nuns who considered forsaking their vows and marrying. In a letter to three nuns who were considering leaving the cloister for marriage; Luther unfolds the two grounds for abandoning convent life and monastic vows. The first relates to nuns who were put in the cloister as children and did not make vows for themselves. On the second ground, "flesh," Luther writes the following:

> Although women are ashamed to acknowledge this, Scriptures and experience teach us that there is only one in several thousand to whom God gives the gift to live chastely in a state of virginity....Just as eating, drinking, waking, and sleeping are appointed by God to be natural, so God also wills that it be natural for a man and a woman to live together in matrimony. This is enough, therefore, and no woman need be ashamed of that for which God has created and fashioned her.[74]

In his typical pattern, Luther claims the authority of Scripture and experience to bless what was officially condemned by the church authorities.

Luther described Genesis 2:22 ("And God brought her to Adam") as "a sort of description of betrothal."[75] It is important to him that God brought Eve to Adam, making God the author of the marriage. Luther connected this to Christ's command in Matthew 19:6 ("What God has joined, let no one part"). It is on this basis that Luther claimed the "lawful joining of a man and a woman is a divine ordinance and

---

73. Oberman, *Luther: Man Between God and The Devil*, 274.

74. See Martin Luther, "Letter To Three Nuns," in ed. and trans. Theodore G. Tappert *Luther: Letters of Spiritual Counsel,* The Library of Christian Classics, vol. 18, eds. J. Baillie, J.T. McNeill, and H.P. Van Dusen (Philadelphia: The Westminster Press, 1955), 271.

75. Luther, "Lectures on Genesis 1-5," 134.

institution."[76] He offered continual pastoral care and comfort to those who struggled over whether to marry. At the wedding of the dean of the cathedral of Merseburg, just a year before his death, Luther preached:

> for the comfort of all those who are in the married state, that they be emboldened and encouraged. If all of you [who] are married are not rich, as not all of you can be rich, then be satisfied with what you have, and let it be your strong consolation that you have been married in accord with divine ordinance, and be assured that God will keep watch over this his ordinance and blessing.[77]

With this foundational piece of Luther's view in place--that sexuality's drives are natural and intended to serve God's ordinance and blessing through marriage-I now move to Luther's understanding of marriage as a civil estate and the ground of all political authority.

Marriage as a Civil Estate

In keeping with the shift from marriage as a sacrament to marriage as an estate outlined above, Luther worked out a fresh understanding of marriage as God's divine ordinance in creation; that is, in the civil realm. Because, for Luther, the fall stole the original human ability to know and live in communion with God and God's will, humans do not recognize God's (left[78]) hand in the estate of marriage working to constantly create and uphold the world. A brief side trip into Luther's understanding of God's two-fold rule is imperative here, for outside of

---

76. Ibid.

77. Martin Luther, "Sermon at Marriage of Sigismund Von Lindenau (1545)," ed. and trans. John W. Doberstein, *LW* 51, 362.

78. Luther spoke of God's creative and preserving work on the left (estates, civil realm) and God's redemptive work on the right (callings, ecclesiastical realm). See Lazareth, ed., *The Left Hand Of God: Essays on Discipleship and Patriotism* (Philadelphia: Fortress Press, 1976), xvi and passim. Marriage exists as a part of the creative and preservative work of God, but can become a calling, a place where Christians work out faith-activated love for their neighbor, which relates to God's work on the right hand.

his understanding of God's rule Luther's view on sexuality and marriage makes little sense.

Luther's discussion of marriage is not the typical place to look for an understanding of public life, but, as will become clear, this is by far the most appropriate place. In explaining Matthew 19: 3-9, a discussion of the grounds for divorce, Luther discusses the law of Moses:

> God established two types of governments; he gave two types of commandments. Some are spiritual, teaching righteousness in the sight of God, such as love and obedience; people who obeyed these commandments did not thrust away their wives and never made use of certificates of divorce, but always tolerated and endured their wives' conduct. Others are worldly, however, drawn up for the sake of those who do not live up to the spiritual commandments, in order to place a limit upon their misbehavior and prevent them from doing worse and acting wholly on the basis of their own maliciousness. Accordingly, he commanded them, if they could not endure their wives, that they should not put them to death or harm them too severely, but rather dismiss them with a certificate of divorce. This law, therefore, does not apply to Christians, who are supposed to live in the spiritual government. In the case of some who live with their wives in an un-Christian fashion, however, it would still be a good thing to permit them to use this law, just so they are no longer regarded as Christians, which after all they really are not. [79]

Three points must be drawn out immediately in order to make clear what Luther intends with this view of the two governments. First, God established and presently rules through both governments, worldly and spiritual, although by different means (law and gospel) in each. Second, every Christian lives under both governments, for all Christians are righteous and sinful at the same time. Third, even though the two governments are to be distinguished (neither separated nor equated); nonetheless, they constitute "complementary expressions of God's creative and redemptive activity."[80]

---

79. Luther, "The Estate of Marriage," 31.

80. Lazareth, *Luther on the Christian Home,* 110-111. On this point, Lazareth is clear and helpful, but perhaps not as nuanced as Luther's own views. As German theologian and Luther scholar Gerhard Ebeling notes, "It is true that on thorough examination much more careful differentiations will

Luther always worked out these ideas in relation to specific issues. His intention was not an abstract theory but proper description of God's world as he understood it. He saw the Church's assertion of temporal power in the papal bull *Unam sanctam* (1302)[81] as completely wrong, and his efforts were directed at reestablishing the proper place of temporal authority as part of God's intention for the preservation of the world. These two governments can be correlated with Luther's basic view of the distinction between God's law and gospel, but even more fundamentally, this view was grounded in a New Testament eschatological view of the two ages, Adam and Christ.[82]

As a way to assist people in the civil or temporal work of ruling the world and fighting the devil's destructive work, Luther believed that God had mercifully "established the natural orders[83] which counteract the wiles of the devil and guide the destructive forces within man into constructive channels thus making orderly life possible."[84] Through human work in these orders, God continues to create and preserve the

---

have to be made in relating the distinction between the two kingdoms to the distinction between law and Gospel. Nevertheless, the co-ordination of the one *regnum* with the *lex* and the other *regnum* with the Gospel is fundamental." Ebeling "The Necessity of the Doctrine of the Two Kingdoms," in *Word and Faith*, trans. James W. Leitch (Philadelphia: Fortress, 1963), 389; another more recent and very sophisticated treatment of these themes is Oliver O'Donovan, *The Desire of the Nations: Rediscovering the Roots of Political Theology*. (Cambridge: Cambridge University Press, 1996), esp. 193Ff.

81. Steven Ozment, *The Age of Reform*, 20. Ozment writes that in the papal bull *Unam sanctam* (1302) "Pope Boniface VIII boldly asserted the Church's temporal powers against the kings of France and England and triggered the most serious confrontations between Church and state in the Middle Ages."

82. Lazareth, *Luther on the Christian Home*, 108.

83. The German word here, "*Stände*" is translated "office" or "estate" as well as "order."

84. Forell, *Faith Active in Love*, 113. Aside from Forell's excellent treatment of this topic, a recent, concise and quite accurate discussion of these ideas is Carl E. Braaten, "God in Public Life: A Rehabilitation of the Lutheran Idea of the 'Orders Of Creation'," in *Encounters With Luther*, Vol. 4: Lectures, Discussions and Sermons at the Martin Luther Colloquia 1985-1989, ed. Eric W. Gritsch (Gettysburg, Pennsylvania: GAM Printing, 1990), 232-250; Reprinted in *First Things* 1:8 (December 1990): 32-38.

world, although to the eyes of the world, God is hidden. Luther wrote that "the blind world, because it does not know God and his work, concludes that it is owing to its own cleverness, reason, and strength that a community or dominion endures and thrives."[85] Even though God's work is all around, people do "not acknowledge him even though they bump their heads against [God's work]."[86] Luther uses a favorite way to talk about God's work in and through the estates or orders in his instructions to all kings, princes, councilmen, and those in authority about how to govern and keep the peace:

> [Those in authority] should proceed as if there were no God and they had to rescue themselves and manage their own affairs; just as the head of a household is supposed to work as if he were trying to sustain himself by his own labors . . . He should regard all such preparation and equipment as being the work of our Lord God under a mask, as it were, beneath which he himself alone effects and accomplishes what we desire.[87]

As though under a mask, God works through humans using their reason and conscience--by which one could know a sort of "natural" law which God has written on all human hearts--in the various orders.[88]

---

85. Martin Luther, "The Exposition of Psalm 127, For The Christians at Riga in Livonia (1524)," trans. Walter I. Brandt, *LW* 45, 328.

86. Ibid., 329.

87. Ibid., 331.

88. Luther's views on natural law are the source of great debate in the 20th century. For Luther, "natural law" meant all people "have a certain natural knowledge implanted in their minds (Rom. 2: 14-15), by which they know naturally that one should do to others what he wants done to himself (Matt. 7: 12). This principle and others like it, which we call the law of nature, are the foundation of human law and all good works." Martin Luther, "Lectures on Galatians 5-6 (1535)," *LW 27*, 53. Luther felt that the clearest expression of the natural law or law of the heart was the Mosaic ceremonial law--the Ten Commandments. Even so, it is not binding on Christians as the Mosaic law, but only insofar as it approximates the law written on the heart. Cf. the fine article by John T. McNeill, "Natural Law in the Thought of Luther," *Church History* 10 (1941): 211-227; also Carl E. Braaten, "Reflections on the Lutheran Doctrine of the Law" in *The Lutheran Quarterly* 18:1 (February 1966):72-84. According to William Lazareth, "Luther could not possibly have meant by this term what it had traditionally stood for in

For Luther, three basic orders or estates existed as general structures of community organization which may take various forms depending on their actual place in a specific culture and historical moment. This relates directly to Luther's view of God's work through humans, as if through a mask, in the work of creation and preservation of the world. Luther outlines the three "orders" at their beginning in the first chapters of Genesis:

> After the church has been established, the household government is also set up, when Eve is added to Adam as his companion. Thus the temple is earlier than the home, and it is also better this way. Moreover, there was no government of the state before sin, for there was no need of it. Civil government is a remedy required by our corrupted nature.[89]

Within these three general "orders"--church, family, and government--Luther found many useful and important places where one can work in ways which serve the community and bring greater peace and justice into the world.[90] This possibility existed because of the high view Luther gave to reason and conscience in the civil realm.

---

the Aristotelian categories of Roman Catholic moral philosophy." Lazareth adopts Gustaf Aulén's term, "law of creation," in an effort to set Luther's language in his view of God's two-fold rule of the world. Christians, insofar as they are redeemed, obey the law of Christ or the law of love, which is to say they need no law. But, insofar as one is not redeemed, and all people in the world share alike in this, to some extent "bear within their hearts in however distorted and corrupted a form a knowledge of the law of their creator. Persons in rebellion no longer possess a saving knowledge of God, but they still have consciences which witness to the contradiction between right and wrong." See Lazareth, *The Left Hand of God*, 123-127.

89. Luther, "Genesis 1-5," 103-4. By household government, Luther means much more than our modern concept of the nuclear family; he means the entire domestic economy, and here he draws directly from Aristotle: "in German we call 'managing the household' [*Haushallten*]; just as Aristotle writes, '*Oeconomia*,' that is pertaining to the household economy which comprises wife and child, servant and maid, livestock and fodder." Luther, "Psalm 127," 322.

90. See the brief but helpful summary by William H. Lazareth, "Orders," in *The Westminster Dictionary of Christian Ethics*, eds. James F. Childress and John Macquarrie (Philadelphia: The Westminster Press, 1986), 441.

Reason, viewed negatively by Luther theologically, receives his highest praises insofar as it works through the three orders to bring peace in the temporal realm. The work of everyday life lived in service to neighbors, of which marriage was part, *could* be managed fairly well without faith. Luther writes:

> Involving other people, man is rational enough to act properly and needs no other light than reason. Consequently, God does not bother to teach men how they are to build houses, or make clothes, or marry, or make war, or sail a boat. For all such matters, man's natural light is sufficient. But in divine matters, such as man's relation to God and how God's will is fulfilled for our eternal salvation, here man's nature is completely stone-blind.[91]

Because of reason's inability to follow God's will, Luther was clear-minded enough to see that some distinction must be made between the "office" or "order" and the person filling it. God's intention that there be structures through which humans may order life together does not mean that all particular orders will be beneficial for life and health; history is full of the use and abuse of order by excessive power and privilege.

Therefore, even in the secular realm, Luther sees the limits of reason, and thus the "orders" are even more important. As discussed in the first of the two major shifts above, Luther laments the way reason will set up for itself all sorts of special ways to please and appease God, thereby despising the very places through which God's preserving power is working. In other words, Luther was not at all convinced of human ability to actually use reason and conscience for the good of the community but rather believed that humanity usually abused both for the good of oneself. Luther's hard realism about human sinfulness was the major reason Luther thought the orders or estates were of such importance. Still, any argument that these orders are so static that human creativity and effort cannot change and improve them simply does not do justice to Luther's views, broadly considered. Karl Holl writes that:

91. Luther quoted in and trans. by Lazareth, *Luther on the Christian Home,* 117.

> the idea that Luther regarded the orders of the world as a natural law, to be accepted by the Christian in the same way as the wind and the weather, is as remote as possible from his real point of view. Although they have reference to natural (i.e., God-ordained) relationships, the secular orders themselves are for Luther human (i.e., changeable) institutions that are capable of being improved.[92]

With this cursory detour through Luther's core views on the civil realm, a context emerges for both understanding his comments on marriage as a civil estate and as the ground of all political authority.

Luther finds the creation of marriage in God's action in Genesis 2:18 ("The Lord God also said: it is not good that man is alone; I shall make a help which should be before him"[93]). In bringing Eve to Adam, Luther says Adam was made complete because together they could bring about God's good intention: the procreation and preservation of humanity. Now, after sin has changed our nature, marriage also provides some structure to human relationships, both in terms of companionship and in terms of a sexual partner.[94] Luther had no illusion that marriage exists solely among Christians (as shown above in his rejection of marriage as a sacrament). Its existence in the civil realm means that "it also has the sanction and praise of the heathen, in accordance with the judgement of reason."[95] Luther argues that because "marriage is an outward, bodily thing...[and because] I eat, drink, sleep, walk, ride with, buy from, speak to and deal with a heathen, Jew, Turk, or heretic, so I may also marry and continue in wedlock with him."[96] Any non-Christian, in civil terms, was to be regarded and respected; they are "just as much a man or a woman--God's good creation--as St. Peter, St. Paul and St. Lucy . . ."[97]

---

92. Holl, *The Reconstruction of Morality*, 132.
93. Luther, "Lectures on Genesis 1-5,"115-116.
94. Ibid.
95. Martin Luther, "Lectures on Genesis, Chapters 21-25," trans. by George V. Schick, *LW* 4, 232.
96. Luther, "The Estate of Marriage," 25.
97. Ibid. I do not mean to ignore the awful and regrettable things Luther said on the basis of theological views about Jews, Turks and other non-Christian people. I aim to show here that in terms of the civil realm, he often praised the "heathen" and "pagan" peoples for their wise construction

Luther believed that the estate of marriage could not only be found across cultures, but that it preceded all estates. Reflecting on the origins of marriage, Luther wrote in a wedding sermon that "this holy estate and divine ordinance of marriage . . . is the oldest of all estates in the whole world; indeed, all others are derived from that estate . . . ."[98] This high praise is largely because of the role parents have in the care and nurture needed to raise children. In the Large Catechism (1530), Luther sums up much of his fully developed view in his comments on marriage as a part of the Sixth Commandment:

> It is a glorious institution and an object of God's serious concern. For it is of the highest importance to him that persons be brought up to serve the world, promote knowledge of God, godly living, and all virtues, and fight against wickedness and the devil.
>
> Therefore I have always taught that we should not despise or disdain marriage, as the blind world and the false clergy do, but view it in the light of God's word, by which it is adorned and sanctified. It is not an estate to be placed on a level with the others; it precedes and surpasses them all, whether those of emperor, princes, bishops, or anyone else. Important as the spiritual and civil estates are, these must humble themselves and allow all people to enter the estate of marriage, as we shall here. It is not an exceptional estate, but the most universal and the noblest, pervading all Christendom and even extending throughout all the world.[99]

Luther's view of marriage as a decidedly civil yet God-intended estate had profound ramifications for social life in 16th century Germany.[100] The focus on an estate whose authority "precedes and surpasses" all other authorities and in which children would be "brought up to serve the world" led Reformation scholar Steven Ozment to call Luther's view of the estate of marriage "the cradle of citizenship."[101]

Marriage as a Christian Calling

---

of society.

98. "Sermon on the Marriage of Sigismund Von Lindenau (1545)," translated and edited by John W. Doberstein, *LW* 51, 358.

99. Luther, "The Large Catechism," *BC*, 393.

100. Witte, *From Sacrament to Contract*, 53-70.

101. Ozment, *When Fathers Ruled*, 9.

In order to apprehend Luther's full view, however, one more step must be taken. Luther hints at this in the long quote on the Sixth Commandment above when he says, "I have always taught that we should not despise or disdain marriage, as the blind world and the false clergy do, but view it in the light of God's word, by which it is adorned and sanctified."[102] The blind world does not see God's presence in the estate of marriage; it is only through the eyes of faith, viewed in the light of God's word, that a person sees the divine nature of God's work. The estate does not change when seen through the eyes of faith; rather, the person is transfigured through God's forgiveness and lives out faith-activated love toward the neighbor.

Luther makes it clear that the estate does not change but that it is being "in Christ" or "in the Spirit" which teaches one "how to live a Christian and godly life in that estate."[103] According to Luther, "to recognize the estate of marriage is something quite different from merely being married."[104] One who does not recognize God's word and work behind the estate cannot but become bitter and complain at the drudgery. In a delightful and detailed example, Luther compares the view of natural human reason and the perspective of a Christian to the duties of a husband and father:

> Now observe that when that clever harlot,[105] our natural reason takes a look at married life, she turns up her nose and says, 'Alas, must I rock the baby, wash its diapers, make its bed, smell its stench, stay up nights with it, take care of it when it cries, heal its rashes and sores, and on top of that care for my wife, provide for her, labor at my trade, take care of this and take care of that . .

102. Luther, "The Large Catechism," *BC,* 393.

103. Luther, "The Estate of Marriage," 35.

104. Ibid., 38.

105. Luther used imagery from scripture which is based on a correlation between patriarchal stereotypes of women and things he considered bad. Although it is anachronistic to apologize for Luther--he did much to improve the plight of women in his day-- I recognize that by my reproduction of that language I reinforce age-old sexist stereotypes. I hope that by being true to what Luther actually said, more help may come to women from his ideas about creation, redemption and the Christian life such as in the quote above than damage because of his problematic metaphorical usage.

> . and whatever else of bitterness and drudgery married life involves? What, should I make such a prisoner of myself? O you poor, wretched fellow, have you taken a wife? Fie, fie upon such wretchedness and bitterness! It is better to remain free and lead a peaceful, carefree life; I will become a priest or a nun and compel my children to do likewise.'
>
> What then does the Christian faith say to this? It opens its eyes, looks upon all these insignificant, distasteful, and despised duties in the Spirit, and is aware that they are all adorned with divine approval as with the costliest gold and jewels. It says, 'O God, because I am certain that thou hast created me as a man and hast from my body begotten this child, I also know for a certainty that it meets with thy perfect pleasure. I confess to thee that I am not worthy to rock the little babe or wash its diapers, or to be entrusted with the care of the child or its mother. How is it that I, without any merit, have come to this distinction of being certain that I am serving thy creature and thy most precious will? O how gladly will I do so, though the duties should be even more insignificant and despised. Neither frost nor heat, neither drudgery nor labor, will distress or dissuade me, for I am certain that it is thus pleasing in thy sight.'[106]

Although, Luther concludes, the world might judge this humble father "an effeminate fool" for his mothering role in the family, because he is acting in the Spirit, God and all the hosts of heaven are smiling.[107]

The term "calling" or "vocation" ("*Beruf*") are most often used to describe the work of a Christian in his or her particular place in God's estates.[108] Whereas all people, including Christians insofar as they are still sinners, participate in God's estates, Christians also are alive "in Christ" so that their participation in daily work changes because of their inner motivation. Through life "in Christ," a Christian regards God's will to be whatever the needs of her neighbors are wherever she lives and works. The "ordinariness" of this view of Christian life brought Luther again and again to affirm that humans "co-operate and

---

106. Luther, "The Estate of Marriage," 39-40.

107. Ibid., 40.

108. The key work on the concept of calling in Luther's work remains Gustaf Wingren's *Luther on Vocation*, trans. Carl C. Rasmussen. Philadelphia: Muhlenburg Press, 1957.

help [God] with his work."[109] The corollary of this active faith is freedom; few rules are needed because through liberty "in Christ," a Christian finds confidence and strength to act creatively for the neighbor.[110]

The freedom of a Christian, therefore, means that while one is bound to serve the neighbor in love, one has the responsibility to decide how a course of action might be most fruitfully pursued in a given life situation. Karl Holl reflects that there is

> here in the context of everyday life a manifestation of that creative action which Luther pointed to as the epitome of morality, namely the art of sensing what the situation demands, according to the 'genius of the heart,' and thus to replace rigidity with the flexibility of life.[111]

This creative living out of faith in everyday life, when applied to the relation between two people in marriage, resulted in "the home be[coming] a 'warm-up in love', which made possible a more skillful exercise of love toward others."[112]

Aware that the devil causes trouble even for the Christian, pulling the desires of the heart in all directions, Luther offers a strategic practice which trains the "genius of the heart" to know what it is to do and how it is to love. By attention to care of the self, Luther argued, one finds an exemplary model for how to care for others:

---

109. Luther quoted in and trans. by Lazareth, *Luther on the Christian Home*, 145.

110. Luther often commented that no rule should be given but evangelical freedom be exercised in faithful love toward the neighbor. See Luther's words to a husband about how to deal with his wife in their life together:

> Now it is impossible to give a rule for this. God leaves it to everyone to treat his wife considerately according to each wife's nature. You must not use your authority arbitrarily; for you are her husband to help, support, and protect her, not to harm her. It is impossible to set specific bounds for you. Here you yourself must know how to proceed thoughtfully.

Luther, "Sermons on the First Epistle of St. Peter (1523)," trans. Martin H. Bertram, *LW* 30, 92.

111. Holl, *The Reconstruction of Morality,* 133.

112. Ozment, *The Age of Reform,* 389.

> Now, you can stand it when your body emits a stench before you realize it, or when it festers and becomes pussy and completely pollutes your skin. You make allowances for all this. In fact, this only increases your concern and love for your body; you wait on it and wash it, and you endure and help it in every way you can. Why not do the same with the spouse whom God has given you, who is an even greater treasure and whom you have even more reason to love? For love among Christians should be the same kind of love as that of every member of the body for every other one, as St. Paul says (Rom. 12:4,5; I Cor. 12: 12-26), each one accepting the faults of the other, sympathizing with them, bearing and removing them, and doing everything possible to help him. Hence the doctrine of the forgiveness of sins is the most important of all, both for us personally and for our relations with others. As Christ continually bears with us in His kingdom and forgives us all sorts of faults, so we should bear and forgive one another in every situation and in every way.[113]

For Luther, then, a proper approach to marriage followed Christ's love for the world, giving himself for it, and thereby offering forgiveness and new life. But if this means of learning is too lofty, one can look to practical lessons found in concern for oneself to learn what is required for care of one's spouse. Most of all, Luther thought, growth and practice in love were required in marriage, as in the Christian life. Through such practice in love and forgiveness, marriage could become a "school for character" where the marriage partners, bound to forgive and love the neighbor as themselves, learn most of all, then, to love the nearest of neighbors, their spouse.[114]

Interpreting Luther Today

This chapter sketched an outline of how Luther's revolutionary theological insights and advice on the Christian life came out of an eminently pastoral perspective. Luther's distinctive views on embodiment, creation, sexuality, and marriage unfold in the larger development of his views on God's world, both the civil realm and the

---

113. Martin Luther, "The Sermon on the Mount (1532)," trans. Jaroslav Pelikan, *LW* 21, 98.

114. Bainton, *Here I Stand*, 235.

spiritual realm, both law and gospel. In particular, these views can be noticed in two major shifts in Western Christianity's relation to sex and marriage: from a two-tiered Christian life to one obedience of faith for all Christians, and from marriage as a sacrament in the ecclesiastical realm to marriage as an estate governed by the civil realm. However, because God is the one who creates and rules (civil realm) and who redeems and sanctifies (ecclesiastical realm), God is lord of both. Moreover, these two realms are never to be separated or collapsed, but rather distinguished carefully. Only the Christian lives in both the civil realm and its estates--including marriage--and yet transforms those estates "in Christ" by faith toward God and loving service to the neighbor. These positive effects Luther intended and worked hard to implement throughout his life. In conclusion, it is also important to ask what unintended effects Luther's revolution might have had that live in our late 20th century context.

An intended and yet unintended effect could be described as locking sexuality up in marriage between a man and a woman. Luther remarked that there are three categories of people who need not marry; he bases these three on Christ's comments about the three eunuchs (Matt. 19:12). The three include those who are impotent from birth, those who become so during their life, and those rare few who are able to be celibate for the sake of the Kingdom. "Apart from these three groups," Luther wrote, "let no man presume to be without a spouse. And whoever does not fall within one of these three categories should not consider anything except the estate of marriage."[115] Luther's ideas, in their context, constitute a remarkable witness and affirmation of sexuality and marriage. He struggled to respond to the crisis of his time. However, as the next chapters will show, this Reformation linking of sexuality to marriage between a man and a woman has come to be used as a weapon against many gay and lesbian Christians who struggle with issues of sexuality outside of the marriages officially blessed by the Church. Ironically, the ELCA today employs Luther's teachings on marriage to enforce law-based requirements of celibacy for the priesthood!

115. Luther, "The Estate of Marriage," 18-19.

Chapter 3

The Heterosexual Structure of Creation: The Orders of Creation in American Lutheranism

United States Lutherans employ certain interpretations of Luther and the "Reformation heritage"[1] in responding to variously perceived social crises over sexuality in church and society. Changing social mores regarding such divisive issues as divorce, contraception, abortion, sexual expression outside of marriage, and homosexuality parallel a growing number of official United States Lutheran church pronouncements on these topics beginning in the 1930s and increasing in frequency through the 1950s and 1960s.[2] U. S. Lutherans, at least

1. I bracket this term because it is used by some theologians today (Cf. Lazareth, below) as if such a thing as the "Reformation heritage" were clear to all, a view I argue against. Rather, I aim to show that any monolithic view on the "Reformation heritage" is a rhetorical construction used in the politics of contemporary debates.

2. The traditions of United States (U.S.) Lutheran social teaching mix with the history of U.S. Lutheran mergers. Briefly, the Lutheran Church in America (LCA) and the American Lutheran Church (ALC) both had significant traditions regarding social statements. I explore these two traditions (including their antecedent bodies) as they provide background to the Evangelical Lutheran Church in America (ELCA). The Association of Evangelical Lutheran Churches (AELC), the third body which joined the LCA and ALC to form the ELCA, was itself a break-off from the Lutheran Church-Missouri synod (LC-MS). LC-MS had no social statements until very recently, although they did carry on a lively debate about social issues in their main synod German and English periodicals, *Der Lutheraner* and the

since the 1940s, have appealed to some form of the troublesome Lutheran idea of the "orders of creation"[3] as a basic method of linking God's intention in sexuality to the social institution of marriage. The debate over the content and meaning of this key piece of "Reformation heritage" underlies current struggles over sexuality in the ELCA. Not surprisingly, debates for the last forty years center on this exact point, some wanting a restrictive application of the idea in order to hold out against societal change, and others, rejecting the simple appropriation of another generation's theological work, aiming at open-ended reexamination of central theological positions. Despite the serious challenges to this central position (alternatively described as "the order of creation," "the structure of creation," "God's design in creation," "the heterosexual structure of creation" and other mixtures), it remains at the center of the official church position.

Lutheran Witness. The LC-MS history did not significantly influence the directions taken by the ELCA. For more on the LC-MS and social issues, see Alan Graebner, "Birth Control and The Lutherans: The Missouri Synod as a Case Study," in *Women in American Religion*, ed. Janet Wilson James (Philadelphia: University of Pennsylvania Press, 1980), 229-252. I rely primarily on official church pronouncements and statements, but attention must be paid to the individual works of certain theologians. The Lutheran teaching theologians of the last thirty years have had an immense influence on the process of developing, and often writing, the social statements to be considered. In most cases I will distinguish between official church statements and individual works, but often the lines between the two blur.

3. The term comes from the German, *Schöpfungsordnugen*, which was first used by 19th century German theologian Gottlieb Christoph Adolph Harless (b.1806) who influenced a generation of German theologians who depended on this concept (Werner Elert, Paul Althaus, Walther Künneth, Friedrich Gogarten, and Emil Brunner). Some, including Althaus and Gogarten, used this interpretation of Luther to defend the state as autonomous unto itself, ordained by God, and on this basis justified their support of the Nazism and Hitler. Although Luther never used the word *Schöpfungsordnugen*, he used other expressions including the terms natural order, divine order, etc. The problem emerges when Luther's sense of the orders' historicity is lost and the orders of a particular time and place can claim legitimation in some mythical time. Carl Braaten comments that "Acknowledging the historicity of the command of God addressing all people in the common associations of life should at least discourage every ideological absolutization of quite transient formations of life." See Carl E. Braaten, "God in Public Life," 235.

Order of Creation: An Unchangeable Norm?

Representative of the mood in some parts of the ELCA today, William Lazareth claims that this central but highly ambiguous and contested idea of the "orders of creation" now exists as the "unchangeably normative" remains of the "Reformation heritage." A brief look at Lazareth's position quickly shows how one (influential[4]) leader in the ELCA now speaks in these normative terms. In the fall of 1994 he published a three page introduction to a re-printed edition of the last chapter of his 1960 book, *Luther on the Christian Home*. He claims that when he wrote the book in the 1950s his target was "loveless legalism;" he now wishes to employ "the Reformer's sex and marriage ethic" against an "antinomian license" especially as he sees that represented in the ELCA's first draft of a statement on human sexuality.[5] He asks "what remains unchangeably normative" as a part of his effort to exclude any possibility of supporting or blessing same-sex unions--a possibility the first draft of the social statement recommends for church discussion.[6] Lazareth claims his "normative church doctrine" dictates that Lutherans "should not condone the sinful

4. Lazareth's work as a teaching theologian seems "to influence the church's life at almost every level--worship, teaching, ecumenical relations and social statements." See Timothy F. Lull, "LCA: A Church Called Lutheran," *The Lutheran*, December 1987, 13.

5. William H. Lazareth, "ELCA Lutherans and Luther on Heterosexual Marriage," *Lutheran Quarterly,* 8 (Autumn 1994): 235-7.

6. It is worth noting that the use of normative language has shifted in the discussions of a Lutheran sex and marriage ethic. This is helpfully shown by Lazareth's writing practice--his first paragraph in the 1994 article is nearly a word for word reprint from his 1979 article titled "Luther on Sex, Marriage, and Family," in *Marriage in Crisis,* eds. George W. Forell and William H. Lazareth, (Philadelphia: Fortress Press, 1978), 58-64. The few words changed by Lazareth for the reprint are quite instructive. Instead of seeing the present as "an age that is growingly characterized by *lustful* license (1979, p. 58)," now he sees "an age that is growingly characterized instead by *antinomian* license (1994, p. 235)." Additionally, whereas he asked "*what is* that Reformation heritage? (1979, p. 58)," he now asks "*what remains unchangeably normative in* that Reformation heritage? (1994, p. 235)."

acts (conduct) of an intrinsic disorder (orientation) in God's heterosexual ordering of creation."[7]

In this chapter, rather than proving the existence of a normative position among U.S. Lutherans, I detail ***how*** what Lazareth and others now talk about as normative--marriage seen as God's heterosexual ordering of creation--came about historically in fits and starts, constantly competing with other subtly and substantially different options. Mapping the historical relationships between various statements and stages of church debate undermines Lazareth's effort to claim an "unchangeably normative" view of sexuality in the Reformation heritage. Through close examination of the most important discussions and statements of the last forty years, the nuances in the arguments behind churchly statements on the subject come to light.

The chapter's major sections first trace two churchly paths, the ULCA (1930s - 1950s) in and through the LCA (1960s - 1980s) as well as a parallel look at the old ALC (1930s - 1950s) in and through the ALC (1960s - 1980s). In each of these, I show the central influence of the "orders" theology but also attend to the growing openness to view marriage in alternative ways, in part because of an increasingly open perspective on change in sexual ethics. While specific statements on homosexuality remain negative, the context and content of these negative statements become more tentative and contested, a fact poorly recognized in the polemical debates--exemplified in Lazareth's position above-- in the ELCA currently. I conclude the chapter with a brief discussion of the ELCA's own efforts to produce a social statement on sexuality that would, among other things, come to agreement on the status of gay and lesbian people, their committed relationships, and especially their fittedness for ordained ministry.

The Unlikely History of the "Unchangeably Normative"

Lutheran Church in America

A major influence on the shape of U.S. Lutheran social ethics began in the early 1940s when Paul White, a ULCA pastor in the New York Synod, initiated a study group among area pastors. Known as the

7. Lazareth, "Heterosexual Marriage," 235-7.

"Timotheans," this group met monthly to present papers members had prepared on social ethics. One member, Harold C. Letts, was to become (in 1946) the Secretary for Social Action with the Board of Social Missions. In his interview for that position, Letts was asked by Dr. Franklin Clark Fry if he thought Lutheran theology supported social action. Letts responded that it did, but that "it hasn't been illuminated or clarified."[8] Fry commissioned Letts with beginning a process to clarify a particular evangelical and theological approach to Lutheran ethics.

The goal of the process was worked out in the Committee on Faith and Life, which in its report to the 1948 ULCA convention called for a:

> scholarly study, which may eventuate in a definitive book, of the Lutheran approach to Christian social responsibility. This book should bring together and clarify the full teachings of Scripture on this subject, the witness of our confessions thereto, and all the pertinent pronouncements of the U.L.C.A. Its chief purpose would be to school Lutherans in the Scriptural and confessional grounds for social action.[9]

By the 1956 convention, Letts could report on the impending publication of a three volume work titled *Christian Social Responsibility*, made up of essays by many of the leading U.S. Lutheran theologians and ethicists of the day.[10] With its publication, Letts declared, "A basic step in the building of an evangelical and constructive social action program for the ULCA is nearing completion."[11] *Christian Social Responsibility*, by the structure of the

---

8. I rely on the excellent work of Christa R. Klein with Christian D. von Dehsen, *Politics and Policy: The Genesis and Theology of Social Statements in the Lutheran Church in America* (Minneapolis: Fortress Press, 1989), 31ff.

9. The United Lutheran Church In America, *Minutes of the Sixteenth Biennial Convention, Philadelphia, Pa., October 6-14, 1948* (Philadelphia: The ULCA Publication House, 1948), 302.

10. Authors included Letts, Joseph Sittler, William H. Lazareth, Martin J. Heinecken, Harold Haas, E. Theodore Bachmann, Jerald C. Brauer, Rufus Cornelsen, Karl H. Hertz, Howard Hong, Franklin Sherman, T.A. Kantonen, Charles W. Kegley, and Theodore G. Tappert.

11. The United Lutheran Church In America, *Minutes of the Twentieth Biennial Convention, Harrisburg, Pa., October 10-17, 1956* (Philadelphia:

topics dealt with in each of the three volumes, set a pattern characteristic of the ULCA and later LCA social action studies and statements. The pattern moves from a *descriptive* look at the present social situation (Vol. One, *Existence Today*) to a *normative* discussion of confessional and biblical sources (Vol. Two, *The Lutheran Heritage*). Then a *regulative* conclusion offers pragmatic application for Christian life today (Vol. Three, *Life in Community*).[12]

Letts' efforts have profoundly shaped discussion among Lutherans in the United States since that time (of course, the primary effects were felt first in the ULCA and the LCA, then more recently in the ELCA). More specifically related to my argument, the chapter on marriage and sexuality from this collection, titled "Christian Faith and Family Life" by Harold Haas, set the tone and language for official positions on sexuality up to the present. In 1956, as Haas was finishing his doctoral work at Drew University in Christian Sociology, he received an appointment as Secretary of the Board of Social Missions. This appointment serves both as an indication of Haas' significant influence during the 1950s but also serves as a harbinger of things to come--Haas served as the first Executive Secretary of the LCA Board of Social Ministry, continuing to be a central influence throughout the 1960s. Haas' work deserves critical attention because of the language he introduced, especially the language of a "heterosexual structure of creation" which has taken on significant rhetorical weight today in the writing of Lazareth and others.

In the brief introduction, Haas grounded his argument in the basic structure of Christian ethics worked out by Joseph Sittler in the first essay in the same volume.[13] Following Sittler, Haas asserted that all "Christian ethical decisions must ultimately be grounded in the redemptive and restorative deed of God in Christ."[14] The person's relationship with God determines the way one engages the facts of a given situation, which in turn leads to the form and nature of the ethical decision. This faith active in the particular situation does not obey a

The ULCA Publication House, 1956), 1121-2.

12. Klein with von Dehsen, *Politics and Policy*, 35.

13. Joseph Sittler, "The Structure of Christian Ethics," in *Christian Social Responsibility, Vol. III, Life in Community,* ed. Harold C. Letts (Philadelphia: Muhlenberg Press, 1957), 3-39.

14. Harold Haas, "Christian Faith and Family Life," in *Christian Social Responsibility*, ed. Letts, 149-50.

preset pattern. Quite the opposite, Haas argued, because on this faith basis one cannot "set forth universally binding laws which will always predict what the response of faith will be to any given set of facts."[15]

Haas' article followed the three-fold pattern established by the three volumes of *Christian Social Responsibility*. His argument began with a descriptive section, "Marriage and Family in Contemporary Culture," in which he aimed to lay out a realistic view of the state of marriage and the family in the 1950s. Citing the large movements of industrialization and urbanization, Haas saw a basic shift occurring from home-centered life with low mobility and homogeneous mating to fragmented life of high mobility and heterogeneous mating. One fruit of these changes, "the movement of feminism has served to refute in practical demonstration that women are in any area of life inferior to man. It has helped remove legal, social, and economic shackles from women."[16]

The new status of women, Haas claimed, led to "certain ambiguities" which have burdened marriage and the family in our culture. In a quotation that helps immeasurably in evaluating Haas' choice of theological sources (normative section) and the practical suggestions (regulative section), he continued:

> In ignoring some of the meaning of the created structure of heterosexuality, there has been a de-emphasis of the difference between man and woman. This has resulted in a tendency to set up men and women in modern society as competitors. There has been a devaluation of the role of homemaker . . . Moreover, the effect on children, as well as on marriage and family, can be seriously deleterious. [17]

His distaste for the social effects of feminism serves as an example of the "--isms" which Haas placed in his litany of the excesses of modern society (others were individualism, hedonism, secularism, and materialism). His prognosis upon finishing the "descriptive" section simply stated that social changes have produced "a crisis in both marriage and family."[18]

---

15. Ibid., 150.
16. Ibid., 153.
17. Ibid., 153-154.
18. Ibid., 157.

To this crisis, Haas posed the question of the underlying nature and purpose of marriage and family, the central question of his normative section, "Marriage and Family in the Christian Faith." In order to answer his question in terms of the Christian faith, Haas wrote, "It is necessary to first come to grips with the significance of the underlying structure of heterosexuality and of its expression in sexual union."[19] Through collapsing the two Genesis creation accounts, Haas argued that the creation accounts are not about individuals, but the "bi-unity between man and woman."[20] Additionally, male/female sexual differentiation has the purpose of establishing among humans a unique type of community. Haas does not stop at biological complementarity; social changes related to the excesses outlined above drove him to claim a metaphysical complementarity. "Within this earthly existence, revelation of part of the mystery of being can occur to the man through the woman and to the woman through the man. This is part of the givenness of creation."[21]

The biological and metaphysical sex drive brings male and female together into a community, and within that community both find the fulfillment of their being. The fact that women tend to nurture family and men tend to provide sustenance and protection finds its roots in creation. Each maintains the spiritual dignity which God has given alike to both man and woman. Haas willingly granted equality of the sexes in God's eyes--that would not cause social disruption. He had different advice for worldly life. Spiritual equality between God, men and women ". . . does not mean that they are to strive to be alike. Man and woman were created to be complementary to each other, in their togetherness to constitute a created whole."[22] Because this complementary structure of creation leads to a union, Haas next considered the significance of sexual union.

Sex as given by God is good. Haas argued that by its very nature, the sexual union "always involves the whole person and is revelatory of one's very being, it establishes a basic union between a man and a

---

19. Ibid., 159.

20. Ibid., 160.

21. Ibid., 160-161. For this argument, Haas depends on the work of Derrick Sherwin Bailey and Otto Piper. It becomes imperative for his theory of sexual union below.

22. Ibid., 162.

woman. For good or ill, there is a fusion of persons that takes place in an act of sexual intercourse."[23] In Haas' logic this fusion led to the related claim that sexual union "can find full and free expression only in the 'one flesh' relationship which is the ontological basis of marriage."[24] Although this is what God intends the sexual relationship to be, sin has distorted this community. Through Christ, however, the possibility exists for restored relationship: "the more life becomes a re-enactment of God's deed in Christ, so much the more can his blessing be channeled through the structure of heterosexuality."[25] Marriage arises, according to Haas, from these two facts of creation: heterosexuality [sexual differentiation] and sexual union.

Four rubrics guided Haas' discussion of the nature of marriage: (1) one flesh union, (2) structure of creation, (3) calling, and (4) indissolubility. The first, one flesh union, finds bases in Genesis 2.24 and Mark 10.8, and provides the means for each person to find completion in another. The one flesh union, as a structure of creation, provides the basis for the sociological institution of marriage. In the second, drawing on Luther's argument against marriage as a sacrament, Haas argued that sexual desire, which drives male and female toward one flesh union, finds direction and regulation in marriage as a structure of creation.[26] In the third, as Haas follows Luther, the redemptive power of God in Christ Jesus transforms the believer so that marriage becomes a Christian calling, the locus of neighbor love, and the center of Christian community. Because both the Christian and the non-Christian enter into marriage, this aspect of marriage marks the uniqueness of Christian marriage. Lastly, indissolubility of marriage contained two basic components. Marriage within the intention of God consists of a lifelong permanent relationship between one man and one

---

23. Ibid., 165. For Biblical support, Haas draws on I Cor. 6: 15, but relies on other contemporary theologians (Bailey and Piper) for the interpretation of St. Paul.

24. Ibid., 167.

25. Ibid., 168.

26. Haas used Luther's argument for marriage as a "remedy against sin." This is not necessarily negative, Haas wrote, for it honestly recognizes the strength of the sex drive and the real damage it can do through abuse. For this reason, marriage can be seen as a constructive structure to direct passions toward the faithfulness, peace, and joy of God's vision of human life. Ibid., 172-173.

woman. This marriage, then, produces fundamental changes in the partners which cannot be altered.

Haas ended the essay with the regulative section of the essay entitled "Christian Ethical Decision and Problems of Family Life." He argued that "it is a function of the Christian faith to stand in judgement toward aspects of culture that violate something as fundamentally rooted in creation as marriage and family."[27] Haas chose three "areas of moral decision" to discuss, all of which are at least implicit in the previous two sections. The first, "divorce," was of long-standing concern to the church (see discussion of 1930 and 1956 ULCA statements on marriage and divorce below). Haas argued that in God's intention, marriage is indissoluble but with human sin, many marriages do in fact end in separation and divorce. Haas suggested that only through repentance and forgiveness can remarriage be entertained.[28]

The next two areas of "moral decision" were titled "responsible parenthood" and "the problem of working mothers." In the first, Haas saw the danger of uncoupling sex from the necessity of reproduction with the mass introduction of contraception because "the sexual relationship might be used both within and outside marriage simply for personal gratification."[29] Against this fear, Haas had constructed an elaborate, metaphysical view of one flesh union-as-fusion in an effort to buttress an argument against promiscuity. In a footnote, Haas admits that this fusion cannot be proved, but nonetheless must be asserted in order to buttress the church's ethical argument against pre-marital or extra-marital sex. He further encouraged responsible family size and parenthood. In the second area of moral decision, Haas worries that the "combination of financial pressure and drive for status" causes wives and mothers to take jobs outside the home. He raised two ethical

---

27. Ibid., 175.

28. Importantly here Haas drew on Luther in order to point out that one should not make an absolute or binding law against remarriage. Haas writes: "Luther taught that no general principles or particular verses of the Bible could be applied to all situations indiscriminately. Rather it is necessary to examine each individual case in terms of what is demanded by peace and good order and how the law of love can be fulfilled." Ibid., 180. This case by case way of dealing with life dilemmas indeed has its foundation in Luther, and it is a fruitful place to engage the tradition in working out new directions for sexual ethics.

29. Ibid., 182.

problems; first, that the mother-child relationship strains and breaks under the pressures of the work world, and second, that thereby the fundamental nature of woman will not be centered where it should--in "wifehood and motherhood."[30]

Although many things could be said, I will offer two interpretative comments on Haas' argument at this point. First, although some of Luther's writings can be found to support the basic points of Haas' arguments, I do not believe these capture the place in which Luther was most constructive, nor the place in which he can most help the church today.[31] Haas' emphases show a bias toward Luther's emphasis on the civil and biological nature of marriage, especially with the focus on his idea of "orders" rooted in the Genesis creation story. Additionally, Haas' arguments toward a metaphysical or ontological one flesh union as the basis for marriage are simply not arguments found in Luther. In agreement with the medieval church, Luther felt that the vow of fidelity, promised by two people to each other, constituted the basis of marriage.

Second, Haas' use of "the heterosexual structure of creation" language has nothing to do with homosexuality, as it comes to be employed later (as the example of Lazareth above clearly shows). In other words, for Haas, the heterosexual structure of creation is a rhetorical construction employed to emphasize that men are men and women are women, and God intends them to stay that way. Haas employs the language in two ways; first, in an awkward attempt to force culturally constructed gender roles back into the original creation against the feminist efforts at equality, and second, in an effort to make male-female sexual union somehow revelatory of the mystery of being in order to respond to a perceived threat, given the growing availability of contraception, of pre- and extra-marital sex.

In the same period of time that Haas was writing the essay "Christian Faith and Family Life," the ULCA Department of Social Action reviewed a 1930 statement on Marriage and Divorce[32] and prepared a

30. Ibid., 183.

31. The conclusion to chapter two above gives hints about creative use of Luther along these lines, whereas chapter five will deal with the subject more thoroughly.

32. See the Report of the Committee on Moral and Social Welfare in The United Lutheran Church In America, *Minutes of the Seventh Biennial*

revised study and statement at the 1954 convention for the review of pastors. The study and statement were drafted by a committee of laity, pastors and professors and presented for adoption at the 1956 convention. According to historian Christa Klein, Haas and his article for *Christian Social Responsibility* were "the guiding spirit behind the statement which condenses his argument and draws upon his language."[33] Because it mirrors Haas' argument so closely, I will not summarize the entire argument, but simply point to three places where the argument clearly shows its dependance on Haas' formulations.

The following examples are consonant with, but not actually stated as such in, Haas' work, and refer to Luther's problematic idea of the "orders." In the first case, while neither the study nor the statement use Haas' exact language, the structure of creation argument is first applied to homosexuality. According to the study, homosexuality constitutes "one of the most common types of sexual deviation," "a denial of God's intention in creation," which because it is not "in unity" with the procreative purposes of sexual expression should be viewed counter to the "fundamental structure of creation."[34] Second, the statement conflates Luther's use of the term "orders" and contemporary Lutheran efforts to capture the meaning of "orders" by the use of the term "structures". Then, it states that one easily defined structure is sex differentiation. Luther surely recognized sex differentiation; it was not, however, one of the three "orders" (see chapter two). Third, the study wrongly calls monogamy an order of creation. Again, Luther praised monogamy and felt that the promise of fidelity constituted marriage yet he did not view monogamy itself as an order of creation. These

---

Convention, Milwaukee, WI, October 7-14, 1930 (Philadelphia: The ULCA Publication House, 1930), 103-112. The study and statement are notable in two respects; first, the problem is clearly divorce--one of the ten pages is devoted to marriage, the others to divorce--and second, that marriage has a two-fold function--one civil ("the divinely appointed way for the establishment and maintenance of the family") and one spiritual ("one of life's great schools" which "can be made to develop character according to the will of God").

33. Klein with von Dehsen, *Politics and Policy*, 54.

34. This resonates with Haas' use of "the heterosexual structure of creation" language. See "Marriage and Family Life, Report of the Board of Social Missions" in The United Lutheran Church In America, *Minutes of the Twentieth Biennial Convention, Harrisburg, PA, October 10-17, 1956* (Philadelphia: The ULCA Publication House, 1956), 1137-1138.

examples show the way an "order of creation" argument was marshalled against threats of social change and how often these arguments were new constructions, not accurate retrievals of Luther's own views.

However, the remarkable spirit of evangelical freedom present at times in Haas' work also shaped the ULCA study and statement, attested to by the presentation of the statement at the convention. Upon presentation of the statement at the convention, The Rev. William C. Zimmermann, chairman of the committee responsible for the statement, told the assembly that the committee had "endeavored to follow the Word of God in the light of true Biblical exegesis." He immediately modified that statement by cautioning the assembly on behalf of the committee: "Mindful that the whole polity of our United Lutheran Church is not one of legislative operation, nor of the establishment of a canon law, we have been careful to avoid any such implications both in the study documents and in the summary statements."[35] For the ULCA, Luther's strong emphasis on Christian liberty acted as a counter so that despite the push for rules on sexuality based on the order of creation arguments, they could not finally say "it *must* be so." Thirty-five years later, the ELCA used the same arguments to create policy that indeed says, "it must be so." (See chapter four).

At least in part because of the careful work done on this statement, it was adopted as an interim teaching statement by the LCA at their 1964 convention. They had tried to draft a statement quickly, but found the task too difficult, and so combined the temporary adoption of the ULCA statement with the creation of a process through which to develop a new LCA statement with hopes that it would be ready for presentation at the 1966 convention.[36] The struggle to create and adopt this new study ("Sex, Marriage, and the Family") was to become so contentious that it was not passed until 1970, a full eight years after the first committee began work on it. One historian included it as one of "three social statements [which] probably tie for first place in the

---

35. Ibid., 1184.

36. See "Marriage and Family Statement, Report of the Board of Social Ministry" in The Lutheran Church In America, *Minutes of the Second Biennial Convention, Pittsburgh, Pennsylvania, July 2-9, 1964* (Philadelphia: The LCA Board of Publication, 1964), 480.

intensity of floor debate at LCA conventions."[37] I now turn to a look at the development of this statement, the only one on the subject created and passed by the LCA.

The contentiousness over the writing of the document was singularly theological. When the Board of Social Ministry realized that a sound and serious study process could not be carried through in time for the 1966 convention as originally planned, they created an extensive time line leading to a statement in 1968. This revised time line began with the preparation of three working papers for the consultation of the board through 1965. The new statement was to reflect the changing understandings of human sexuality in the social sciences; therefore, two of the working papers reflect this (one from a pastoral counseling perspective and one from sociology). Whereas most of the committee agreed with what these papers described as the situation in church and society, Carl Braaten's theological paper divided the group on how to respond theologically to the situation.[38]

One contemporary Luther Theological Seminary professor described the social situation thus: "Everything nailed down is coming loose."[39] The terms "the new morality" and "situation ethics" flew around like popcorn in a pan of sizzling oil.[40] Many board members advocated for a new direction in interpreting the Lutheran view of the family as an "order of creation." Braaten's position represented a more conservative position, typical of the work Haas had done in the previous decade.

---

37. Richard J. Niebanck, "LCA: Church in the World" *The Lutheran*, December 1987, 27.

38. Klein with von Dehsen, *Politics and Policy*, 106-7. I do not have access to Braaten's actual paper, "Sex, Family and Marriage," which was not published. However, on the basis of comparison between quotes in Klein's discussion, and the two published discussions of these topics by Braaten in the 1970s, a close approximation can be made to the argument presented in 1965. His article of 1979, "Sex, Marriage, and the Clergy" contains extensive autobiographical reflections about the process of the consultation on "Sex, Marriage, and Family" and his differences of opinion with the committee, as well as sections that are word for word from the paper presented in 1965.

39. James H. Burtness, "The New Morality: Some Biographical Comment," in *dialog* 5 (Winter 1966): 10.

40. Cf. Joseph Fletcher, *Situation Ethics: The New Morality* (Philadelphia: The Westminster Press, 1966).

Braaten's "ontological-normative" method drew certain supporters, but according to historian Christa Klein, many "preferred a more 'situationalist' approach 'born of a concern that the ethicist take with utter seriousness the questions of contemporary man before offering answers to them'."[41] The inability of the board to bring a document to the 1968 convention can be traced directly to this theological controversy.

Braaten raised the question of what distinctive teaching the Christian faith can offer regarding sexuality. He first stated that human sexuality is good, a part of God's creation. Braaten's position explicitly responded, as did Haas' before him, to the feminist movement and its critique of gender inequality within marriage. Braaten wrote, "It is possible to blaspheme the Creator by denigrating the dignity and goodness of human sexuality in its differentiation between male and female."[42] He grounded this threat of blasphemy in the ontological argument which ultimately moved the committee to look elsewhere for their theological framework:

> The image of God in human beings is reflected in the sexual differentiation between male and female. A single human being cannot reflect the image of God, for if God is love, it implies a relationship in God between the lover and the beloved. Sexuality is the means by which God has built into man and woman to drive them out of isolation toward a mutually fulfilling love. The bi-polarity of the sexes belongs to the basic structure of human existence.[43]

---

41. Klein with von Dehsen, *Politics and Policy*, 107. Klein's quotes are from the LCA Board of Social Ministries Minutes.

42. Carl E. Braaten, *Eschatology and Ethics: Essays on the Theology and Ethics of the Kingdom of God* (Minneapolis: Augsburg Publishing House, 1974), 165.

43. Carl E. Braaten, "Sex, Marriage and the Clergy," *dialog*, 18 (Summer 1979), 170. Along these lines, in *Eschatology and Ethics*, Braaten claims "Men will never be satisfied with woman too much like themselves; they would rather find their fulfillment with women who retain their unlikeness--*ex oppositio*." 172-3.

So, for the first time, the position Haas initiated regarding "the heterosexual structure of creation" connects directly to the *imago dei,* the divine image implanted in our being at creation.

Braaten uses Freudian notions of libido and insatiable sex-drives to speak of the effect of sin on God's good creation. The libido drive toward self-satisfaction ultimately ends in self-destruction. Braaten's answer to this drive lies "within the structure of monogamous marriage."[44] This structure, called an "order of creation" means "that marriage is as much a part of God's intention for man and woman as for the lilies to grow in the field or for the birds to fly in the sky."[45] The gospel can transform the gift of marriage so that the partners may share in God's healing agapic love. In this situation, the mystery of covenantal and divine love moves marriage toward its height.

By the beginning of 1969, the Commission on Marriage working on the study finally broke with Braaten's perspective and went in other theological directions. Floyd Martinson, lay member on the commission and sociologist responsible for the first section of the final study, remembers that "we went through a lot of theologians until we found the kind we wanted. We were looking for a theologian who could develop a love-based, relational evangelical ethic over against code morality."[46]

Serving as editor of the final report, Cedric Tilberg worked with Haas to revise a lengthy draft of the theological or normative section provided by theologian and consultant Martin Heinecken. Under the guidance of William H. Lazareth, the board's committee on marriage prepared a social statement based on the longer study. Although on the whole the statement follows the study closely, the statement introduces the language of "the heterosexual structure of God's creation" in the section dealing with homosexuality, language which the study never introduces even in its section on homosexuality (I return to this below).[47] After passage at the 1970 biennial convention, both the

---

44. Braaten, "Sex, Marriage and the Clergy," 171.

45. Ibid.

46. Klein with von Dehsen, *Politics and Policy*, 108.

47. The statement reads, "Scientific research has not been able to provide conclusive evidence regarding the causes of homosexuality. Nevertheless, homosexuality is viewed biblically as a departure from the heterosexual structure of creation." *Sex, Marriage, and Family: A Contemporary Christian Perspective,* ed. Cedric W. Tilberg (New York: The

statement and the study were published as *Sex, Marriage, and the Family: A Contemporary Christian Perspective* in a volume in the Christian Social Responsibility series. Because of the efforts of the commission to take a new direction in dealing with the "orders" in relation to contemporary society, this study merits close attention.

The introduction to the study acknowledges the difficult and perplexing problem of Christian address to contemporary experience of sex, marriage, and the family. The committee knew this perplexing reality as a result of their study of the culture's changes, yet this difficulty even more clearly reflects the difficulties of the eight years spent in their own deliberations. Given these struggles, they framed the study as "deliberately limited in scope and tentative in style."[48] Under the challenges presented by vast changes in the culture, the authors admit that the church itself has revised some of its historical positions on ethical issues (e.g., divorce and contraception). Carefully, they lay out the process through which these revised positions have come about, which they characterized

> neither as a repudiation of past judgements nor merely as a response to changing public opinion. Rather, it is due to two things. First, it is a serious attempt to get at the fundamental concepts and relationships that lay behind earlier judgements. Second, it is a recognition that the context of aspects of human life can change so radically that specific ethical judgements must sometimes be turned upside down if their essential meaning is to be preserved.[49]

This remarkable statement summarizes the difficult and courageous reflection undertaken by the commission. They were undertaking a theological task "in a far more profound sense than that of applying accepted concepts and formulations to new social situations. Theological concepts and formulations are themselves part of the necessary investigation."[50]

The first section, drawn from Martinson's initial paper on contemporary cultural issues, emphasizes the relationship between talk of a "new morality" and the "separability of sex, marriage, and the

Lutheran Church in America, Division for Mission in North America, 1970), 12.

48. Ibid., 17.
49. Ibid., 18.
50. Ibid., 19.

family." The possibility of this separation--which results from a combination of widely available birth control, the growing social and economic independence of women and the average life span growth--means that the basis for marriage shifts from procreation to companionship. Prompted largely by its concern for persons rather than simply upholding structures, at times the church has modified its stance on various ethical issues (e.g. slavery, divorce, contraception).

To respond to these changing views on ethical ideals, the study's second section aimed at seeking "the essentials of the Christian understanding of life and of man and to explicate them in relation to sex, marriage and family as these are experienced in contemporary society."[51] The section begins by sketching a "consensus" view on the issues relating to sex, marriage, and the family which the previous generation had worked out in the years after World War II. This view represented Haas and Braaten's positions, views that the committee no longer believed to be fully useful. In a single generation, such new issues marked the landscape that no consensus existed to be employed in Christian life. On the one hand, some argue for "extreme permissiveness in matters of sex" while on the other hand, a conservative reaction aims "merely to reiterate the old virtues and call for stricter laws and more discipline."[52] But because the formulations of the past are not simply "timeless truths" the committee set this as the direction for the theological chapter:

> Restatement, therefore is constantly necessary; misunderstandings need to be corrected; attempts at enlargement need to be made. Sometimes entirely new approaches have to be developed which, however, do not lose their continuity with the past.[53]

With this bold statement, the study clears the way for just such a new approach.

The new approach moved through four sections: "The Ambiguity of Sex," "Marriage and Family as Secular Reality," "Marriage and Family as Christian Calling," and "The Christian Mode of Ethical Decision." "The Ambiguity of Sex" arises from the tension between sex as part of

---

51. Ibid., 39.
52. Ibid., 44.
53. Ibid., 45.

who we are as God's good creation and its frightful abuse as a result of sin. Sin seen as a relational ill separates humans from a right relationship with God, and therefore with neighbors and the world itself. The sexual role for humans has a great variety of forms across different cultures, but from the Christian perspective this relationship forms in response to God's relation to humans. In this view, sexual intercourse does not join two opposites in an ontological union (as it did for Braaten, and somewhat differently for Haas even earlier). Rather, "the same word 'to know' is used in the Bible for the relation of God to his chosen people (to whom, incidentally, He is everlastingly faithful) as well as for the most intimate union of the sexes."[54]

Sexuality ideally leads to a faithful relationship. In the second section, "Marriage and Family as Secular Reality," the general view of marriage as faithful relationship finds grounding in the work of God the Creator. Though many humans do not recognize God's work, marriage and family are structures of God's created order aimed at the preservation of human community. The argument immediately qualifies the use of this language of the structure of creation redirecting the reader away from any sense that the structure remains static throughout the centuries. Rather, there "is a dynamic quality about creation. It cannot be apprehended only in terms of what once occurred. It must also be perceived in terms of what now is and what seems to be emerging."[55] The development of this line of argument led to a definitional statement of marriage from a theological point of view; "A life-long covenanted union of one man and one woman, based on fidelity, is indicative of the creator's intention for a cradle of community."[56] This statement should not glorify a certain form, however. The emphasis lies "deeper than form; it focuses on the quality of the interrelationships. Although form is always important in human life, it is, however, less important than the dynamics of interrelationships."[57]

The focus on qualities of relationships leads the authors into the third section dealing with "Marriage and Family as Christian Calling." Here the tensions of the committee over theological issues take center stage. The section begins with an acknowledgement that two competing

---

54. Ibid., 47.
55. Ibid., 49.
56. Ibid.
57. Ibid., 50.

views exist. The first, and the one represented by Braaten above, identifies one flesh union with sexual intercourse and in its very nature changes the participants on an ontological level. However, on the basis of the widely divergent sexual practices in various cultures around the world, the conclusion drawn in the first perspective holds little promise for any sort of empirical verification. The second finds a center in God's covenant relation with Israel in the biblical witness. Following from that, the "essence of marriage is that two people voluntarily take each other and promise fidelity."[58] In the specific context of these relationships, Christians can respond to their calling by God to serve their neighbors. In the family, a person experiences a school in community helping to develop the skills which are a part of loving another. The goal cannot be simply to uphold the typical middle class family given the changes in society. Christians are called to work creatively; in these times, "who knows what new patterns of family living may emerge under the guidance of God's spirit?"[59]

Some guides for working in creative times emerge in the last section on "The Christian Mode of Ethical Decision." This mode fundamentally derives from a way of living in the faith-relationship--it cannot be separated from the law but is never reduced to a code morality or an ethic of principle. A prime example, according to the study's view, lies in Luther's explanation of the Ten Commandments in his Small Catechism. Everything rests on the introduction to the Ten Commandments, which "is not a commandment but proclaims the gracious action of God to which the Christian is expected to respond. This sets up the right God-relation of trust, proper fear, and love, and out of that kind of relation all human conduct is to flow."[60] The concern in this view "will not be to justify oneself but to seek the genuine well-being of the other."[61] Therefore, breaking a "rule" does not constitute a sin; what makes, for example,

> extramarital intercourse a "sin" is not the fact of having sexual intercourse outside whatever the accepted rules for a "legitimate" marriage may be in a given society. Rather, it is that the "sinner" has committed an act, and that there is neither the proper fear and

58. Ibid., 52.
59. Ibid., 55.
60. Ibid., 61-62.
61. Ibid., 62.

> love of God nor regard for the fellow human being involved (not only the partner in the sexual intercourse, but others who are deeply affected.)[62]

The text goes on to say that "the homosexual should not be judged a 'sinner' because of his homosexuality, but because he is a 'sinner' in the same way that everyone else is, viz., because he is alienated from God, self, neighbor, and the world."[63] As such, the sinner is still accountable for her or his acts, but the author of the study pounds home the message that no one is righteous but by the forgiveness and mercy of God; therefore, no one has access to moral high ground. This contextual theological position relies on a high level of personal responsibility in relation to the community in which responsibility is lived out.

The study's theological and ethical grounding is then applied to various current issues such as premarital sex, homosexuality, divorce, interreligious marriage, abortion and sex education in the last chapter of the study, "Sex, Marriage, and Family: Some Current Issues." Within the last chapter, the discussions of marriage and sexuality more generally are applied in a discussion of homosexuality. The study states that homosexuality is found in many kinds of persons, far beyond stereotyped images. Further, research has show that sex crimes and emotional disturbance are no more common among homosexuals than among heterosexuals. Summing up their findings on science and homosexuality, the study writes that

> Scientific research has not been able to provide conclusive evidence regarding the causes of homosexuality. Nevertheless, in the last decade or two, the attitudes of churchmen have been changing noticeably, largely under the impact of increased knowledge coming from the disciplines of psychology and sociology, medicine and psychiatry.[64]

The study continues by noting that "homosexuality is to be regarded as a deviation from the norms which are expressed in this study. Nevertheless, homosexuals must be seen as persons and treated with

62. Ibid., 62-63.
63. Ibid., 63.
64. Ibid., 76.

justice."[65] Strong language concludes the section urging repeal of laws that make homosexuality a crime and urging greater understanding and acceptance of homosexuals in the church and society at large.

As I noted above, however, the social statement, produced under the direction of William Lazareth, replaces the more open position of the study by inserting the language of "orders of creation" theology. Homosexuality is treated under the first point, "Some Issues Related to Sexual Expression." Here, the statement *begins* by directly quoting the study's language; yet the second sentence introduces a perspective quite different than one finds in the study. The social statement reads: "Scientific research has not been able to provide conclusive evidence regarding the causes of homosexuality. Nevertheless, homosexuality is viewed biblically as a departure from the heterosexual structure of God's creation."[66] Given, the study does regard homosexuality as "a deviation from the norms" expressed in the study; still, the "nevertheless" sentence in the study expresses growing openness in the church on the issue of homosexuality, given new scientific research. The "nevertheless" sentence in the social statement, the document adopted as official teaching of the church, makes the issue sound decidedly more closed.

Such a shift in emphasis may have been a political as well as theological choice on the part of Lazareth, given the long and contentious process leading to the adoption of the statement. The statement offered to the 1970 assembly received hot debate, especially around the topic of the definition of marriage. Many concerns were raised on the relationship between the law, civil and religious, and the covenantal relationship which the statement used as a foundation for marriage.[67] After eight years of struggle and debate, the statement finally passed.

The LCA developed no other major statements on sexuality; however, after a three year process, the Division for Mission published a booklet entitled *A Study of Issues Concerning Homosexuality*. The advisory committee responsible for the study suggested that the church could neither condemn nor praise, nor ignore homosexuality. In its

65. Ibid.

66. Ibid, 12.

67. Klein with von Dehsen, *Politics and Policy*, 112-113.

conclusions, it looked toward the new Lutheran church to begin on January 1, 1988 and advised that:

> the new church undertake a much more comprehensive study of human sexuality and Christian life today. The committee has often sensed the artificiality of studying homosexuality in isolation from the larger questions of sexual feeling and sexual behavior.[68]

A group of published responses to the study uniformly felt that the committee had argued for church movement "in a positive direction, i.e., toward an acceptance and affirmation of homosexual behavior" which none of the authors of the responses agreed with.[69]

These negative responses to *The Study of Issues Concerning Homosexuality* ironically help to make the case for the LCA's growing reluctance to simply condemn homosexuality as a violation of God's heterosexual structure of creation. I show that the phrase was originally employed by Carl Haas against eroding gender distinctions and increasingly liberal views toward pre-marital sex. Soon after, however, it was enshrined in official statements as an explicit rejection of homosexuality. Yet by the late 1960s, such fundamental change was underway in the church and society that the LCA study, *Sex, Marriage and the Family*, came near to a total rejection of such static arguments about creation's supposed binding structure for all times and places. Even the LCA social statement "Sex, Marriage, and the Family," which uses the phrase "heterosexual structure of creation," departs from earlier rhetoric of homosexuality as a denial of God's intention in creation and counter to the fundamental structure of creation. Rather, the LCA statement acknowledges that science has not conclusively found the causes of homosexuality (science was not even mentioned in previous statements); nevertheless, the statement continues, homosexuality is viewed biblically as a departure from the

68. *A Study of Issues Concerning Homosexuality: Report of the Advisory Committee of Issues Related to Homosexuality* (New York: Division for Mission in North America, Lutheran Church in America, 1986), 44.

69. See Wesley Fuerst, John Reumann, Franklin Shermann, Robert Benne, Gilbert Meilaender, and Blanche Jenson, "A Symposium on the LCA's Study of Homosexuality," *dialog* 26 (Spring 1987): 142-148.

heterosexual structure of creation. While these claims by no means approve of homosexuality, when read in the context of the larger study out of which they came, they reflect the growing influence of a more open-minded, contemporary position.

Such a trajectory from clear condemnation of homosexuality to questioning openness characterizes the history of the ALC statements, as well. It is to that story that I now turn.

American Lutheran Church

Of the four church bodies that formed the ALC, only one had a tradition of making national statements on the major social issues of the day.[70] The old ALC, at its 1938 convention, had created a Board of Charities, but through lack of funding delayed calling a director until a decade later when Carl F. Reuss was hired. He was not a pastor, but held a doctorate in sociology, and had responsibility for what by 1948 was called the Board for Christian Social Action. The board, under Reuss, received "responsibility for promoting action by church members in the social order, in addition to continuing to work with the ALC's social service agencies and institutions."[71]

The board began discussions of a statement on the problems of marriage, divorce, and remarriage, with a goal of updating the pastoral guidelines on these issues developed in the 1930s and 1940s. By 1956, the statement finished circulation among pastors and revisions had been made, so it was presented to the convention. *Marriage, Divorce and Remarriage* was to guide pastors in the instruction of their membership, in counselling, and in parish practice in general. The statement's length evenly divides among the three sections, beginning with marriage. Genesis 2:18 opens the discussion of marriage showing "that male and female complete and complement one another."[72]

---

70. The ALC was formed January 1, 1961 through the merger of the German-heritage American Lutheran Church, the Norwegian-heritage Evangelical Lutheran Church, and the Danish-heritage United Evangelical Lutheran Church. The Norwegian-heritage Lutheran Free Church joined the ALC in January 1, 1963.

71. Charles P. Lutz, *Public Voice: Social Policy Development in The American Lutheran Church, 1960-1987* (Minneapolis: Office of Church in Society, The American Lutheran Church, 1987), 2.

72. The American Lutheran Church, *Official Minutes of the Fourteenth*

Following Genesis 2:24, cleaving and oneness are claimed to be the essence of marriage. It is "an institution of divine origin, a part of God's creative order."[73] In terms of the spiritual character of marriage, the unity experienced is a "constant process of becoming, for marriage is not only an institution but also a continuing way of life."[74] The model of Christ and the Church gives marriage the call to life-long fidelity, where wife is subject to husband and the unselfish love of Christ marks the love of each partner for the other. Therefore, the Christian marriage comes into being "through the redemptive love of Jesus Christ and the sanctifying power of the Holy Spirit."[75]

By the time the old ALC was to merge with the new ALC in the first years of the 1960s, the Board for Christian Social Action had created over fifty statements and studies.[76] Because the merger partners did not have such activist traditions, some notable anxiety existed over the ALC positions. As a result, Reuss was asked to write a series of six articles on "The Christian, the Church and Social Problems" for the ELC periodical, the *Lutheran Herald.* "Courtship and Marriage," his third article[77] constitutes an amazingly accurate summary of Harold Haas' article in *Christian Social Responsibility, Vol III, Life in Community*, published only two years earlier.[78] Haas' influence likely contributed to the use of "order of creation" theology in the early 1960s, an influence that waned significantly by the 1980s. It is important to note this, for Reuss directed the variously named offices and boards for social action in the new ALC through 1981, the period during which all but one of the ALC statements on these topics were prepared.

The first of these statements, "Teachings and Practice on Marriage and Divorce," received the accolade "soundly evangelical" when passed

---

Convention held in Blue Island, Illinois, October 4-11, 1956 (Columbus: The Wartburg Press, 1956), 319.

73. Ibid., 319.

74. Ibid.

75. Ibid., 320.

76. For these statements and studies, see *The Christian and His Social Living* (Minneapolis: Board for Christian Social Action, American Lutheran Church, 1960).

77. Carl F. Reuss, "Courtship and Marriage," in the *Lutheran Herald*, 7 April 1959, 6-7.

78. The structure of Reuss' article follows the progression of Haas' article, but does not directly cite Haas' work.

at the 1964 convention. Work began on the statement almost immediately after the merger, and through consultation with seminary faculties and wide circulation of a preliminary draft among clergy, the statement became the guiding "expression of evangelical Christian views."[79] The section on marriage reflected the old ALC statement of 1956 but clearly with the addition and prominent placement of arguments echoing Haas' views about marriage and its "structure [which] rests in the creation of man as male and female (Gen. 1:27)."[80] In its first section on marriage, "The Foundation for Marriage," the statement optimistically suggests that "Christian people will recognize their marital union as belonging to God's order of creation."[81] The following sections on "The Unity of Marriage" and "Love in Marriage" and "Preserving the Marriage" expand on, but do not significantly stray from, the direction of the old ALC statement. Although not explicitly named here, the clear problem being addressed remains consonant with previous statements and with the LCA statements of the same period, namely, the question of the changing value of marriage in society, including the fact of wide-spread divorce.

Two significant studies of human sexuality, one along more traditional lines and one taking a major new direction, shaped the discussions over the next decade and a half leading up to the last ALC statements on sexuality and marriage in the early 1980s. The first of these two studies resulted from the 1964 convention's call for the Commission on Research and Social Action to explore the theme, "The Relevance of My Faith to My Life in Society." The commission singled out human sexuality as an area of major concern. They engaged the Wartburg college faculty, under the direction of Dr. Karl T. Schmidt, to prepare a resource paper. Wartburg President J. W.

---

79. The American Lutheran Church, *Reports and Actions of the Second Convention held in Columbus, Ohio, October 21-27, 1964*, ed. William Larsen (Minneapolis: Office of the Secretary, The American Lutheran Church, 1964), 421,432. I would like to give more history around the construction of the ALC statements, but no detailed history exists, and archival materials which give detailed information are not available to me. This work remains to be done, and would be an important contribution to understanding the ALC's contribution to the ELCA and more generally, the public voice of Lutherans in the United States.

80. Ibid., 433.

81. Ibid.

Bachman appointed Schmidt, head of the Department of Religion, to be the writer. Commission director Carl Reuss, in the introduction, had this to say: "To an age beset by sexual doubts and confusions about a 'new morality' *Sexual Integrity in Modern Society* speaks a realistic, evangelical Christian, word."[82]

In introducing the subject, Schmidt rolls out what has by this time become a well-worn description of "the contemporary situation" in various Lutheran statements on sexuality. He explains what new problems exist in the area of sexuality in his first section, "So What's New?"

> Following are some of the factors: the heightened preoccupation with sex in western society, greater mobility (the car, e.g.), the impact of relativity on ethics which makes for the questioning of all standards and values (a questioning which, however, is not necessarily evil), the increased independence of womanhood, marriage at a later age, improved methods of conception control, the weakening role of the home, and the lessening influence of religion on the ethical standards of our increasingly heterogeneous culture.[83]

The statement puts Genesis 1:27 and Mark 10:6 right up front, defending both the goodness of sex and that it "is indissolubly related to marriage, to the fulfillment of a man's and a woman's lives in the most intimate union and companionship known on earth--physical, social, intellectual and spiritual."[84] Schmidt describes sexual union as an interpersonal action or an action centered in relational experience. Therefore, sexual union cannot be viewed simply as a thing which one takes or leaves. Here he draws on the biblical use of the word "to know" which, rather than suggesting the biological or some other focus, "always stresses the *interpersonal relationship.*" [emphasis in original][85]

---

82. Carl F. Reuss, "Introduction," in *Sexual Integrity in Modern Society* (Minneapolis: Commission on Research and Social Action, The American Lutheran Church, 1966), 2.

83. *Sexual Integrity*, 3.

84. Ibid., 4.

85. Ibid., 6.

In unpacking the content of this interpersonal relationship, Schmidt turns to four "biblical positives" regarding marriage: monogamous union, fidelity in a life-long union, natural love, and agapic love.[86] The three purposes of marriage can be summarized in this order of importance: 1) companionship, 2) coitus (one flesh union) and 3) procreation.[87] In a concise summary statement, Schmidt puts the Christian view this way:

> . . . we have emphasized the biblical view that 'God created them male and female,' that man and woman are to become one in the 'one flesh' union, and that coitus is both the act and symbol of the larger oneness between husband and wife, a oneness 'until death do us part.' It is only in this context that biblically the sexual act is 'natural.'[88]

Although this slip into a defense from "nature" exhibits some resonance to the arguments of Carl Braaten at this same time in the LCA deliberations, Schmidt remains focused on the relational aspects of sexuality and marriage, and primarily uses biblical arguments from Genesis to demand the "indissoluble" tie between marriage and sexual intercourse.

Tellingly, the above concise statement of the "natural" context for the sexual act lies at the beginning of Schmidt's discussion of homosexuality. Here, "natural" arguments in support of marriage return strongly to the foreground. Sex is only considered "natural" in such a "one flesh union" between a man and woman. Both social science and the bible view homosexuality as "sick" and "unnatural." While he urges tolerance and acknowledges the difficulty in finding a "cure" he still proposes that sometimes "understanding, forgiveness, love, and professional care" can prove a corrective. He concludes by suggesting that society must protect minors from homosexuals, but that the church should aim to "deal understandingly and redemptively."[89] The 1966 statement adopted by the ALC convention

86. Ibid., 7-8.
87. Ibid., 18.
88. Ibid., 22.
89. Ibid., 22-23.

entitled, "The Church and Human Sexuality," consisted of a "retitled, sightly amended draft" of Schmidt's study.[90]

A second significant study of human sexuality, one taking a major new direction from the theological study represented by the work of Schmidt and the Wartburg faculty, came out of a long-term University of Minnesota Medical School Program in Human Sexuality. The program at the University aimed at training those in the "helping professions" to understand themselves better as sexual beings with the aim of making them more able helpers for those they work with everyday. In 1970, the ALC entered into an "action research" program under the Division for Service and Mission in America, using the program for clergy training, for marital enrichment seminars, and for education of key lay members. However, in 1976 enough concerns had been raised about the program that the Church Council resolved to thank the Division for Service and Mission for "its courageous exploration into a sensitive and highly significant area of Christian concern"[91] but halted participation until a full- scale review of the work thus far could be carried out. John Spencer, chairperson of the Task Force, lead a comprehensive review between January and October 1977, listening to supporters, critics and representatives of the institutions involved.

Critics worried that the program reflected "inadequate scriptural and theological emphasis and fails to underscore traditional Christian values regarding family and marriage," presented "homosexuality, sex outside of marriage and other variations of sexual behavior as acceptable and normative," and used "films depicting explicitly sexual activity."[92] Positively, supporters found that the program was "informative," provided "opportunity for personal and professional enrichment, encouraging open communication about sexual matters with spouse, parishioners, and clients," heightened "awareness and understanding of

---

90. The American Lutheran Church, *Reports and Actions of the Third Convention held in Minneapolis, Minnesota, October 19-25, 1966*, ed. William Larsen (Minneapolis: Office of the Secretary, The American Lutheran Church, 1966), 490.

91. The American Lutheran Church, *Reports and Actions of the Ninth Convention held in Moorehead, Minnesota, October 18-24, 1978*, ed. Arnold R. Mickelson (Minneapolis: Office of the Secretary, The American Lutheran Church, 1978), 704.

92. Ibid., 708.

persons in special circumstances," and challenged "participants to examine and affirm their religious and ethical values."[93] Though the "action research" project was ended, the final report found that the project had "provided the church with valuable discoveries which should be utilized" and therefore should "report the findings of this action to the church."[94]

The findings, published under the title *Human Sexuality* by the Division for Service and Mission in America, held some remarkable insights bound to affect the unfolding discussions. Before moving to those discussions which lead to the two statements in the early 1980s, a brief look at the content of the findings from the "action research" project are in order. Findings were numbered and listed as concise sentences with commentary underneath each. The third finding, for example, claimed that in order "to promote responsible sexual attitudes and behavior it is important that church people decode and unmask the traditional theological assumptions and biblical interpretations about human sexuality."[95] Under this finding, the commentary challenged such deeply held formulations as "traditional Christian values" by questioning giving credence to a belief simply because it is tradition--e.g., in the South for nearly 50 years black people were traditionally forced to sit in the back of the bus. The commentary on this finding also questions "the Lutheran viewpoint" and "the Bible says" as statements needing clarification and examination for the assumptions which underlie them. Other findings, raising equally difficult and challenging questions, range from noting the connection between sexuality and our understanding of God to the relationship between sexuality, intimacy, and the ministry of healing.

At the same time as the discussions over the "action research" program at the University of Minnesota unfolded, talks were taking place around a draft statement on homosexuality that was requested in 1976 by the general president of the ALC. The process of soliciting responses from the draft, a process undertaken in 1977, led the standing committee on human sexuality to shift plans; instead of a single

93. Ibid.

94. Ibid., 709.

95. *Human Sexuality: The Findings of the Action Research Project in Human Sexuality of the Division for Service and Mission in America* (Minneapolis: The American Lutheran Church, 1978), 6-7.

document on homosexuality, they endeavored to expand the draft and make it part of a revision of the 1966 statement on *The Church and Human Sexuality*. To assist in this process, they undertook to consult with, respectively, various experts in the area of human sexuality, broadly speaking, and six theological professors drawn from the three ALC seminaries (Luther, Trinity and Wartburg). The committee also made extensive use of the findings from the "action research" project as well, and prepared a statement--*Human Sexuality and Sexual Behavior*--for the 1980 convention.[96]

The statement begins by separating being and doing; humans are sexual in all that they are as people, yet in order to make ethical judgements about sexual behavior, they can separate sexuality and sexual acts.[97] The sexual life that a human being is and acts out comes as a gracious gift and sacred trust from God. Human capacity for sexual behavior is "God's design for continuing the race, but also for enhancing joy and renewing the vows of love and marriage."[98] In a remarkable shift from earlier statements, the connection between sexual identity and gender roles loosens, and admits that "differences in the sexuality of individual males and of individual females cover a wide range."[99] The meaning of Genesis 1:27 (the classic scripture quotation for proving the so-called bi-polar or heterosexual structure of creation) opens up slightly--at least in terms of socially constructed gender roles--when the church determines its view on "biblical, theological, historical, psychological, and sociological grounds."[100]

The document finds four foundations and one necessary ingredient for marriage on the basis of its research; they are "trust, mutual acceptance of agreed-upon roles and expectations, community sanction and support, and long-term commitment. Inherent to marriage is sharing the experience of male/female sexual intercourse (1 Cor. 7:2-9)."[101] Based on the first marriage (Gen 1:27) "of one man and one woman, committed to one another in a covenant of lifelong fidelity," the

96. *Human Sexuality and Sexual Behavior* (Minneapolis: The American Lutheran Church, 1980).

97. *Human Sexuality and Sexual Behavior*, 1.

98. Ibid.

99. Ibid., 3.

100. Ibid., 2.

101. Ibid., 4-5.

statement suggests that Jesus cited an "original design" for marriage (Matthew 19:3-6) that sets the standard for relationships today.

Such an argument from design impacted the statement's position on homosexuality, as well. Yet, given the wide range of sources drawn upon in producing the statement, section G., "Considering Homosexuality," represents a significant change from Karl Schmidt's position fifteen years previous. The section opens acknowledging that current scientific opinion agrees that human sexuality exists on a continuum from homosexual to heterosexual and that homosexual behavior takes various forms. On the basis of such scientific input, they distinguish between homosexual identity and behavior, suggesting that "persons who do not practice their homosexual erotic preference do not violate our understanding of Christian sexual behavior."[102] Thus, the statement notes that the church regards the practice of homosexual erotic behavior as "contrary to God's intent for his children." They note that numerous challenges to traditional biblical condemnations of homosexuality were considered in the process of their work; however, they were "not convinced by the evidence presented." After listing the texts that require attention in order to revise traditional biblical condemnations of homosexuality, the statement concludes, "While we see no scriptural rationale for revising the church's traditional teaching that homosexual erotic behavior violates God's intent, we nonetheless remain open to the possibility of new biblical and theological insights."[103] The section concluded with claims that homosexuals need God's grace just as does every human person; furthermore, such common ground as God's children should impel members toward new attitudes on homosexuality as well as efforts to achieve justice and equal opportunity on their behalf in the civic realm.

After significant debate over this section on homosexuality, *Human Sexuality and Sexual Behavior* passed.[104] It received "comment and

---

102. Ibid, 8.

103. Ibid.

104. Numerous motions were made to remove section G, which discusses homosexuality with the aim of further evaluation and study. Judging from the tone of the motions, these interventions revealed disappointment on the part of some who had spent years working on the issues (the statement originally began as a study on homosexuality alone) only to have the statement stop at the point of revising an historic condemnation of same-sex relations. See The American Lutheran Church,

counsel" status, meaning that its only authority rested in its ability to stimulate thought and action by church members as they read and reflected on the issues.[105] This document, more extensive in dealing with the sociological and psychological factors involved in human sexuality than the statement it replaced, marked key shifts in the basic biblical and theological stance taken in1966.

A second statement completed in the 1980s revised the 1964 *Teaching and Practice on Marriage, Divorce and Remarriage.* This document, carrying the same title, passed in 1982 and carried extra weight as a statement of "policy and practice" for the ALC. The 1964 statement was not substantially changed, but merely underwent editorial changes, such as the use of inclusive language when referring to people. As a result, the content need not receive discussion here.

In sum, a marked shift took place in theological work in the ALC on sexuality and marriage in general, and homosexuality in particular. While the "orders" theology so dominant in LCA discussions does not figure as prominently in the ALC, it too moved from a strong focus on marriage in terms of "natural" male-female complementarity and homosexuality as a "sickness" in need of cure, to the last broad statement, *Human Sexuality and Sexual Behavior*, focused more on marriage as an "original design" of "a covenant of lifelong fidelity" and a concerned and sensitive acceptance of homosexual persons. Drawing on a broad range of sources including biblical and theological, but also scientific, the latter statement left open the possibility that their views could be changed on the basis of new biblical and theological insights. Clearly, as the ALC's Tenth Convention showed, the minds of many had already changed. That fact is no doubt reflected in the tone of such rhetoric as this: "Truth, mercy, and justice should impel members of congregations of the American Lutheran Church to review their attitudes, words, and actions regarding homosexuality."[106]

Reports and Actions of the Tenth General Convention held in Minneapolis, Minnesota, October 1-7, 1980. Arnold G. Mickelson, ed. (Minneapolis: The American Lutheran Church, 1980), 975-977.

105. Only "policy and practice" statements could determine ALC institutional behavior. The distinction between authority of statements began at the 1970 convention. See Lutz, *Public Voice*, 11-12.

106. *Human Sexuality and Human Behavior*, 9.

Evangelical Lutheran Church in America

The history of the ELCA echoes with cacophonic voices of debates over sexuality, and especially over the level of welcome and acceptance offered to gay and lesbian members. Lutheran theologian Timothy F. Lull, speaking at an ELCA "free church conference,"[107] remarked that the issue of acceptance of gay and lesbian members "is our hardest issue, our most painful issue, and the one that has driven so much of our debate and our policy in these last seven years."[108] I will not rehearse the ELCA debates in detail here (in part the next chapter takes up this task). Nonetheless, it is valuable to lay out briefly the various key moments in the ELCA effort to produce a social statement on human sexuality.

In the first year of the new church, no less than eight synods officially requested study of human sexuality, "with special references to homosexuality and the ordination of homosexual persons."[109] Beginning in 1989, a task force of seventeen worked with the Division for Church in Society under the directorship of Karen Bloomquist to develop a social statement on human sexuality to be presented at the 1993 Churchwide Assembly. Upon the recommendation of the Division of Ministry, the church leadership placed the issue of the ordination of "homosexual persons" on hold until after the completions of the report on human sexuality (ironically, at this same time, the Division for Ministry was formulating two documents--*Definitions and Guidelines for Discipline* , used for ordained pastors, and *Vision and Expectations*, used with candidates for ordained ministry--that closed

---

107. Charles P. Lutz notes in the editor's forward to the volume which derived from this conference that "free conferences" have a long history among Lutherans in North America. "They were convened without official denominational sponsorship (thus "free"), usually focused on a divisive theological question, and were attended by both laity and clergy hoping to find some resolution." See "For the Battle-Weary: New Hope" p. 2 in Charles P. Lutz, ed. *A Reforming Church . . .Gift and Task: Essays from a Free Conference* (Minneapolis: Kirk House Publishers, 1995).

108. Timothy F. Lull, "Learning Reform from the Reformers," p. 61 in Lutz, ed. *Reforming the Church . . .Gift and Task.*

109. See "Background Material," in *Human Sexuality, Working Draft*, 34.

debate by requiring a life-long vow of celibacy for gay and lesbian ordination).

In 1991 the task force submitted a study document and, after wide spread discussions, published a first draft of a social statement, *The Church and Human Sexuality: A Lutheran Perspective,* in October 1993. A loud and largely negative response followed media headlines such as "Lutheran Report Supports Gay Marriage."[110]

In response, Karen Bloomquist was removed as director of the study and the task force was replaced by a writing team made up of two seminary professors (Walter Bouman and Eric Gritsch) and a pastor (Cynthia Ganzkow-Wold) who were charged with rewriting based on the more than 21,000 responses to the first draft. After some consultation, *Human Sexuality, Working Draft: A Possible Social Statement of the Evangelical Lutheran Church in America with Accompanying Documents* was released in October of 1994. This draft, a revision of the first with new additions, pleased neither those hoping for change nor those holding out for traditional positions. According to Timothy Lull, Lutherans "now confront a draft document that is more conservative in many respects than the careful and concise statements of the ELCA predecessor churches."[111]

Church leaders, anxious to find some firm ground, postponed plans to present a full social statement and asked instead that a "message" on sexuality be presented that would summarize views on sexuality in which there appears to be consensus. The message, adopted in 1996, does not mention homosexuality but rather deals with sexuality generally, single adults, marriage, responsible parenting, divorce, and abuses of sexuality such as adultery, rape, prostitution, etc.[112]

In response to continuing pressure--including from the Metropolitan Washington D. C. And Sierra Pacific synods calling for no less that complete elimination of policies prohibiting ordination for "practicing homosexual persons"--the 1997 Churchwide Assembly voted to refer the question of church policy and practice on the ordination,

---

110. Don Lattin, "Lutheran Report Supports Gay Marriage," *San Francisco Chronicle* (Thursday, October 21, 1993), A 10.

111. Timothy F. Lull, "Learning Reform from the Reformers," 61.

112. *A Message on Sexuality: Some Common Convictions* (Chicago: Department of Studies, Division for Church in Society, Evangelical Lutheran Church in America, 1996) 1ff.

consecration, or commissioning of non-celibate gay and lesbian individuals to the Division for Ministry and that a status report on these deliberations be brought to the 1999 Churchwide Assembly.[113] A report produced jointly by various units of the church--Division for Ministry; Division for Church in Society; Division for Outreach; Division for Congregational Studies; and Commission for Women--reported on-going work responding to the issue. The report's introduction defends the lack of a timetable for settling the issues and argues that God has offered the ELCA a teaching moment during which the church needs to face the difficult task of taking together about these difficult issues in a spirit of "fairness, understanding, wisdom, patience, creativity, and trust in the Lord of the Church."[114] It was presented and accepted at the 1999 Churchwide Assembly.

In the official acceptance action, titled "The Ordination of Non-Celibate Gay and Lesbian Persons," the assembly "acknowledged the deep level of anxiety and anguish felt by many members," pledged to "continue discerning conversations about homosexuality," admitted there is no "timetable for concluding the discussion," and while affirming that "gay and lesbian people, as individuals created by God, are welcome to participate fully in the life of congregations" of the ELCA, nonetheless voted "to decline to propose at this assembly a change in the standards for rostered ministry related to non-celibate gay or lesbian persons."[115]

While one might interpret this as positive intention to deal with the issues head-on, this does not seem to fit the mood of the parts of the ELCA where the issue seems to have been set aside. Again, Timothy Lull: "the situation seems to be as closed on this subject of our church's official policy toward gay and lesbian persons as at any time since I was ordained in 1972. And many in leadership are now saying we've spent enough time on this so that the subject must stay closed as

113. *1997 ELCA Churchwide Assembly: A Brief Summary of Actions* (Chicago: Department for Communications, Evangelical Lutheran Church in America, 1997) 1.

106. This paragraph depends on the *1999 Pre-Assembly Report*, Other Documents, Section V, "Report and Response to 1997 Churchwide Assembly Action."

107. Evangelical Lutheran Church in America, "The Ordination of Non-Celibate Gay and Lesbian Persons (1999), *Churchwide Assembly Action CA99.06.27*. See http://www.elca.org/dcs/elca_actions/ca99_06_27.html

we move on to other issues."[116] Lull cautiously chides the leading generation of Lutheran theologians for serving "up natural law and orders of creation rather than Christian liberation and grace-centered pastoral theology."[117] Representative among these is Robert Benne, a prominent Lutheran ethicist, who was shocked by the "major shift in Christian sexual ethics" represented by the first ELCA study. Shortly after the release of this study, Benne commented that the church should give up searching for a new sexual ethic and instead promote:

> a renewed vision of Christian marriage and family life accompanied by practical ways we might strengthen them. Why is it that homosexual acts are *never* spoken of approvingly in the Bible? It is because the whole heterosexual structure of the order of creation is so deeply assumed. It is no accident, no homophobic neurosis, that homosexuality--as either 'orientation' or action--is seen as a serious departure from God's intentions.[118]

Harold Haas' language, originally employed in the 1940s to fend off the effects of feminism's emancipatory movement out of pre-packaged gender roles, now can be used in the San Francisco Chronicle to promote marriage between men and women, while at the very same time and on that same theological basis, to marginalize and abnormalize gay and lesbian people.

While some may applaud Benne's rally cry for a reinstatement of the "order of creation" theology as a defense of traditional marriage and family life, many Christians join with Timothy Lull who longs "for a church that can welcome lesbian and gay persons and accept them not only as members but also in public ministry where communities will call them."[119] In this chapter I have shown that twentieth century American Lutherans, contrary to voices such as Benne and William Lazareth, have had more and better things to say about sexuality and marriage than is captured in the theology of a timeless "heterosexual structure of the order of creation." Furthermore, I have shown that the

106. Lull, "Learning Reform from the Reformers," 61.

107. Ibid, 63.

118. Don Lattin, "Americans Search for a New Sex Ethic," *San Francisco Chronicle,* (November 29, 1994), A6.

119. Lull, "Learning Reform From the Reformers," 61.

phrase and the "orders" theology behind it have been employed over and over, in response to variously perceived crises in the area of sex, marriage, and the family. The static and regressive tendencies of "orders" theology led theologians and church statements increasingly to qualify and de-emphasize its role, turning instead to such concepts as covenant, fidelity, and relationship to find the core meaning of marriage. These meanings lend themselves much more powerfully to a theology of sex and marriage that could support the sort of church that welcomes and affirms the gifts and ministry of gay and lesbian Christians.

Yet, as the next chapter shows, another perceived crisis in the church's life led to another regressive use of the "orders of creation" aspect of the tradition. I turn now to an examination of the institutionalization of "orders" theology in ELCA policies that require gay and lesbian pastors and candidates for pastoral ministry to vow life-long celibacy.

Chapter 4

Vision and Expectations: Theology and Policy for Exclusion

From the previous chapter, it is clear that despite some diversity in the ways Lutherans have drawn on Reformation resources, the arguments from an "order of creation" theology are most prominent. This is especially true in times of crisis; Timothy Lull has pointed out that "orders of creation" theology serves as an expedient resource for those who wish to maintain the status quo in the face of tidal waves of change and challenge. A conservative response is not necessarily the wrong response to change. In part, the church is by necessity a conservative institution. A central task of the church catholic consists in "telling the old, old story" in ever-changing cultural and historical contexts. And theology needs to say that God's intentions are constant, not simply blowing back and forth with the changing fads of society. Yet such conservative attempts at standing firm in the face of change can risk missing the ever present activity of God who created the cosmos and still can "do a new thing" (Isaiah 43:19).

A central argument of this book as a whole rests on the claim that the contemporary use of "orders of creation" theology to marginalize gay and lesbian Christians and exclude them from leadership indeed misses the present activity of God. The work of the present chapter is to show how, in recent years, the ELCA has followed the pattern of its predecessor churches in responding to crisis with a conservative "orders of creation" response. More centrally, however, the chapter shows the specific effects, both institutional and individual, of such a reassertion of rigid forms of relational theology. This response has had many negative effects on faithful Christians in congregations across the United States, especially those called to ordained ministry. While other ill effects of this reimposition of the "orders" theology would make a similar point, a focus on candidacy processes and the debate over ordination provides a powerful case study in the outcome of recent Lutheran "reformations" of institutional policy and practice.

From its official beginning in January of 1988, the ELCA has struggled with questions of ecclesiastical authority in a "crisis" over sexuality. This crisis came about through the public questioning of the ordination policy regarding "openly gay"[1] candidates for ministry. Resulting from the coincidence of institutional merger forming the ELCA (through the merger of three smaller Lutheran churches[2]) and a major challenge from gay activists during the same month, the response of the ELCA to this crisis constitutes an instructive case study in institutional use of theology in a perceived "crisis" moment. In response to the crisis over ordination a interpretation of a Lutheran view of marriage as an "order of creation," articulated in the 1950s and 1960s, grounded formulation of policies and processes by which all candidates could be examined regarding their sexuality and if gay or lesbian, regarding their commitment to celibacy.

My argument in this chapter moves through four sections. The first section sets up the analysis to follow by quickly discussing some theories of bureaucracy and its use of examinations as a form of discipline. Following this, a second section traces the history of the problem of candidacy in ELCA and the specific form of the problem (ordination of "openly gay" candidates). In the third section, I show how the form of the problem produced the specific forms of the solutions.[3] The historical watchword of the Lutheran tradition--*ecclesia*

---

1. "Openly gay" is language used by the candidates themselves; the church bureaucracy has continually used the terminology "homosexual." This becomes increasingly clear as the chapter unfolds.

2. The three were the American Lutheran Church, the Lutheran Church in America and the Association of Evangelical Lutheran Churches. Together, the three had around 5.5 million members, making the newly formed ELCA the fourth largest U.S. protestant church body.

3. Cf. Michel Foucault, who discussing problemizations said, "it is a question of a movement of critical analysis in which one tries to see how the different solutions to a problem have been constructed; but also how these different solutions result from a specific form of problemization."

reformata semper reformanda (church reformed, always being reformed)--takes on increasingly predictable possibilities as the church re-forms itself as an efficient and effective modern bureaucracy. The last portion of the argument attempts to sketch the institution's new ways of working, especially regarding the developing candidacy process and the use of *Vision and Expectations* as a tool to govern conduct in and through the three examinations of the process (one to gain entrance to seminary, a second at the end of the first year in seminary, where the church "endorses" the candidate or not, and a third in the final year of preparation, where the church "approves" the candidate or not). While at the outset, the examinations are external and occasional, the process is geared to produce candidates who internalize the discipline of examination, questioning themselves as to their adherence to church standards (and most centrally around the question of sexuality).

Bureaucracy and Disciplinary Power

I employ tools from Max Weber's work on bureaucracy and Michel Foucault's work on the "examination" as a specific form of disciplinary power in my analysis of the development of special examinations of the sexual conduct of candidates.[4] This primarily institutional analysis will highlight the special examination, and the processes and policies which support it, as a specific rationality, noting its movement in social practices and its effects for institutional and individual re-formations. Before continuing with an analysis of the case study at hand, I will briefly lay out, surely in too simplistic a way, the basic Weberian and Foucauldian theoretical tools needed for a critical examination of the institutional re-formations undertaken by the ELCA since its inception.

Max Weber's taxonomy of bureaucracy as a constitutive element in

---

See: "Polemics, Politics, and Problemizations: An Interview," *The Foucault Reader*, 389.

4. I more fully defend the view that Foucault explicitly saw himself working out of a critical philosophical tradition that included Weber in my article "Subject to Discipline: Authority, Sexuality, and the Production of Candidates for Ordained Ministry," *Journal of the American Academy of Religion* 66 (Summer 1998): 89-120; see also Arpád Szakolczai, *Max Weber and Michel Foucault: Parallel Life-works* (New York: Routledge Press, 1999).

the development of modernity in various locales sets a larger context for seeing how the ELCA re-formed its ways of working in order to respond to a major crisis of ecclesiastical authority. Weber's work on bureaucracy spans the corpus of his work; only a concise statement of a few grounding ideas relative to his analysis can be introduced here. I will begin where Weber does--with the basic characteristics of bureaucracy: fixed jurisdictional areas ordered by rules, office hierarchy, management based on written documents ('the files'), the presupposition of thorough and expert training, and finally, stable, knowable rules which ground and guide management of the office.[5] From these basic characteristics, Weber aims to show that bureaucracy "has a 'rational' character: rules, means, ends, and matter-of-factness dominate its bearing."[6]

Means and ends indicate the form of rationality for which Weber is most famous: "instrumental rationality." However, Weber's views on rationality are more complex than often noted.[7] The two forms of rationality upon which this chapter depends--formal and instrumental--were regarded by Weber as distinct but inseparable in practice. For example, in discussing the rationalization of the world religions, Weber writes that "[rationalism] means one thing if we think of the kind of rationalization the systematic thinker performs on the image of the world: an increasing theoretical mastery of reality by means of increasingly precise and abstract concepts. Rationalism means another thing if we think of the methodological attainment of a definitely given and practical end by means of an increasingly precise calculation of adequate means."[8] The "formal" or "conceptual" rationality is a necessary precursor for the "instrumental" rationality as the case of the ELCA will show. The rationalization of the norm for sexual expectations for ministerial candidates was both required by and

---

5. Max Weber, "Bureaucracy," in *From Max Weber: Essays in Sociology*, trans. and ed.Hans H. Gerth and C. Wright Mills (New York: Oxford University Press, 1946), 196-8.

6. Ibid., 244.

7. See, for example, Ann Swidler, "The Concept of Rationality in the Work of Max Weber," *Sociological Inquiry* 43 (1973):35-42; Donald N. Levine, "Rationality and Freedom: Weber and Beyond," *Sociological Inquiry* 51 (1981):5-26.

8. "The Social Psychology of the World Religions," 293 in *From Max Weber*.

provided a foundation for the construction of an efficient means of ordering the population of clergy candidates.

Weber explains that the success of bureaucratic organization lies in "its purely technical superiority over any other form of organization." "'Calculable rules' [are] of paramount importance"; the "peculiarity of modern culture and specifically of its technical and economic base, demands this very 'calculability' of results."[9] An effort to carefully manage outcomes raises the question of external criticism. The "administration always tends to be an administration of 'secret sessions': in so far as it can, it hides its knowledge and action from criticism." Weber continues:

> The tendency toward secrecy in certain administrative fields follows their material nature: everywhere that the power interests of the domination structure toward the outside are at stake . . . we find secrecy. If it is to be successful, the management of diplomacy can only be publicly controlled to a very limited extent.[10]

This is especially true with modern media; Weber suggests that the

> extraordinary increase in the speed by which public announcements . . . are transmitted exerts a steady and sharp pressure in the direction of speeding up the tempo of administrative reaction towards various situations."[11]

In order to better manage public speech and use of public forms of media efficiently, a rationalization of education takes place. Schools "are dominated and influenced by the need for the kind of 'education' that produces a system of special examinations and the trained expertness that is increasingly indispensable for modern bureaucracy."[12] These special examinations have existed previously, to be sure, but full bureaucratization brings them to the fore. Weber cautions us about what we might assign as a motivation to the call for the introduction of regular curricula and special examinations in the training of office

9. Weber, "Bureaucracy," 214-215.
10. Ibid., 233.
11. Ibid., 215.
12. Ibid., 240.

holders: "The reason behind it is, of course, not a suddenly awakened 'thirst for education' but the desire for restricting the supply for these positions."[13] Special examinations are a specific function of bureaucratic domination; by its internal logic "examinations irresistibly advance."[14]

Michel Foucault's work on the "examination" as a technique of disciplinary power will add a more specific set of tools to Weber's more general ideas on bureaucracy. In part three of Foucault's study, *Discipline and Punish: The Birth of the Prison*, he details the peculiar operations of what he calls "disciplinary power." "The chief function of the disciplinary power is to 'train', rather than to select and to levy; or, no doubt, to train in order to levy and select all the more."[15] It is an effective and yet subtle power which functions in a "calculated, but permanent economy." This economy works through the "use of simple instruments; hierarchical observation, normalizing judgement, and their combination in a procedure that is specific to it, the examination."[16] Disciplinary power works through these three, and especially the examination, to "make" individuals.

The first instrument, hierarchical observation, exercises disciplinary power through a structure that both allows exacting and coercive observation. Under this rubric, Foucault discusses architecture; attention to spaciality and structure opens up the ways in which institutions plan "for eyes to see without being seen."[17] Foucault then begins to see a whole set of architectures structured:

> to permit an internal, articulated and detailed control--to render visible those who are inside it; in more general terms, an architecture that would operate to transform individuals: to act on those it shelters, to provide a hold on their conduct, to carry the effects of power right to them, to make it possible to know them, to alter them. Stones can make people docile and knowable.[18]

13. Ibid., 241.
14. Ibid., 242.
15. Michel Foucault, *Discipline and Punish*, 170.
16. Ibid.
17. Ibid., 171.
18. Ibid., 172.

In order for the hierarchial observation to work, however, one must insure more than stones conducive to surveillance. The structure of relationships between those being observed and those responsible for observation must both allow continuous and functional surveillance. The structure is "organized as a multiple, automatic and anonymous power, for although surveillance rests on individuals, its functioning is that of a network of relations from top to bottom, but also from bottom to top and laterally."[19] Within such a fluid structure disciplinary power "is everywhere and always alert."[20]

The second instrument, normalizing judgement, operates according to a juridical model dependent on a rule which forms the goal to which each is expected to strive. The observation of how closely each measures up to the norm set for the whole group marks the success or failure of each, approving of the one achieving the mark, and condemning those who fall short. In one sense, homogeneity is imposed, "but it individualizes by making it possible to measure gaps, to determine levels, to fix specialties and to render differences useful by fitting them one to another."[21]

Finally, hierarchical observation and normalizing judgement are central techniques used in the third instrument, the examination. In this highly ritualized practice, the formation of truth comes about by the exercise of power which makes manifest the subjection of those being examined. Foucault details three effects of the examination. In the first, the economy of visibility is transformed into the exercise of power. Traditionally, the one who exercised power was visible and worked control through the fact of that visibility; "[i]n discipline, it is the subjects who have to be seen."[22] The exercise of power works to objectify the person being examined. In the second effect, the examination introduces documentation of the individual. Once reduced to the level of object, the individual is a knowable, analyzable object who has individual features, aptitudes and a history. Documentation highlights this and makes comparison possible between this one and others, as well as whatever normative standard is employed. In the third effect, the examination, with its documents and individual-as-

19. Ibid., 176.
20. Ibid., 177.
21. Ibid., 184.
22. Ibid., 187.

object, can make each individual a "case." The writing by and about individuals does not serve as a biography; the paper trail "is no longer a monument for future memory, but a document for possible use."[23] The individual receives an individuality, a status linked to the measurements, the gaps, the "marks" which make the "case" and are kept in a file.

Foucault concludes by commenting that political theory of the seventeenth - nineteenth centuries (cf. Hobbes) depends on an abstract individual as a part of a representation of society. This is no doubt true, but the individual is "also a reality fabricated by this specific technology of power that I have called 'discipline'. We must cease once and for all to describe the effects of power in negative terms." He claims, rather, that "power produces; it produces reality; it produces domains of objects and rituals of truth. The individual and the knowledge that may be gained of him belong to this production."[24]

The case study to follow confirms this construal: Weber's general views of the nature of bureaucracy combined with Foucault's quite specific analysis of the operations of disciplinary power in "the examination" allow a more fine-tuned and illuminating analysis of the process for producing candidates for ministry in the ELCA. With this theoretical excursus concluded, however hastily, I now turn to the discussion of the candidacy processes.

Producing Candidates for Ordained Ministry

The policies and processes by which people become rostered leaders[25] in the ELCA are spelled out in the *Candidacy Manual*, now in its third edition. It sets out the process through which potential leaders of the church are "approved"[26] or not for various positions, including

23. Ibid., 191.

24. Ibid., 194.

25. Rosters of different categories for the many people who work part or full time in vocations of the church are kept by the secretary of the ELCA. The two categories relevant here are "ordained ministers" and "associates in ministry" both of whom are required to have theological training and to participate in the candidacy process.

26. This is the official term at present, though when the ELCA was formed in 1988, the term used was "certification." As the argument unfolds, I will pay attention to such changes in terminology.

pastoral ministry. Pastoral ministry, the aim of the process for most candidates, itself is a particular technology of power with a specific history and development in the West. Pastoral care imitates the classic "pastoral" form of power, described as a watchful gaze concerned with the care and guidance of the whole flock *as individuals*. This gaze assumes intimate knowledge of each sheep; the techniques of self-examination and guidance of conscience are of paramount importance.[27]

This rhetoric and its technologies of power are central to the operations of the candidacy process, and the language of the *Candidacy Manual* makes this point clearly.[28] The *Candidacy Manual* plays a pedagogical role for all participants in the process and is the basis for scheduled training sessions for those who serve on candidacy committees which carry out the process of "recruitment, preparation and evaluation" of candidates. The Division for Ministry, located in the institutional heart of the church, acts as administrator of the intricate "network"[29] of relations between candidate, congregation, candidacy committee and seminary.

In order to map these intricate networks of relations, I must especially deal with the creation and central institutional use of the document, *Vision and Expectations: Ordained Ministers in the Evangelical*

---

27. It is worth noting that Foucault is not so much raising concerns about actual pastoral care, though he saw potential for abuse there, as well, but primarily the political adoption of this form of power by large-scale institutions as a means of centralized governance and control. See Michel Foucault, "Politics and Reason" in *Michel Foucault, Politics, Philosophy and Culture: Interviews and Other Writings 1977-1984*, ed. Lawrence D. Kritzman (New York: Routledge, 1990), 58-85.

28. For example, in describing the role of the Synod (geographical areas more or less based on the number of congregations present--Alaska is one synod; Minnesota has six) in providing "a duly constituted Candidacy Committee which *oversees the care* of the candidate and which *provides the guidance and supervision* of those seeking to serve" [emphasis mine]. ELCA, *Candidacy Manual* (Chicago: The Division for Ministry, 1994), 8.

29. "The continuing training and support of a strong *network* of synodical and multi-synodical candidacy committees remains an ongoing, central emphasis of the Division for Ministry . . . " [emphasis mine] Cf. The biennial report of the Division for Ministry in the *1991 Churchwide Assembly Reports and Records, Vol. I* (Chicago: Evangelical Lutheran Church in America, 1992), 130.

Lutheran Church in America. *Vision and Expectations* acts as a guide for self-examination on the part of ministerial candidates. This document, developed in part through an effort to institutionalize a response to challenges over the ordination of "openly gay" candidates for ministry, can be seen as a "grid of intelligibility" working to illumine the specific rationalities, historically analyzable practices, and precise techniques of governance by which the ecclesiastical authority and relative order is established.

I borrow the use of a "grid of intelligibility" as an interpretive practice from Michel Foucault. Foucault contrasted his methodological approach to Max Weber's well known use of "ideal types." While "ideal types" consist of generalizations from various empirical data in order to analyze a particular age or movement, Foucault advocated using historically specific apparatuses or programs, such as Jeremy Bentham's Panopticon, because of their various real effects: "they crystallize into institutions, they inform individual behavior, they act as grids for the perception and evaluation of things."[30] Paul Rabinow, an important interpreter of Foucault's work in the United States, picked up this usage and coined the term "grid of intelligibility." Rabinow describes a grid's use in much the same way as Foucault; it is a matter of taking "real schemas and following out their strategic uses--the transformations as well as the resistances they provoked--as a means of illuminating not a whole age but rather its particular nuclei of knowledge and power."[31] By using *Vision and Expectations* as a "grid of intelligibility" I will show how a certain interpretation of a Lutheran view of marriage--based on "the heterosexual order of creation"-- has been used as a norm for the construction and maintenance of an efficient system of disciplinary and exclusionary practices on which ecclesiastical authority and order is constructed.

Former Bishop of the ELCA, Herbert W. Chilstrom, gave a clue to the direction the analysis would proceed. He wrote in the introduction to *Vision and Expectations* that this "document should not be confused with *Definitions and Guidelines for Discipline*. The latter is a juridical document that describes the grounds on which ordained ministers may

---

30. Michel Foucault, "Questions of Method," in *The Foucault Effect*, 81

31. Paul Rabinow, *French Modern: Norms and Forms of the Social Environment* (Cambridge, Massachusetts: The MIT Press, 1989), 12.

be subject to discipline in this church."[32] One of the central ethical issues at stake is exactly that, in contradiction to the official rhetoric, the use of *Vision and Expectations* constitutes a central disciplinary technique for the correct training of ministers.

History of the Problem: Authority, Candidacy and Sexuality

In the January 4, 1989 issue of *The Lutheran*,[33] an article made an effort to characterize the top ten news stories of the first year of the new 5.5 million member ELCA. In selecting stories, the authors tried to gauge not only "what are headlines in the public press--but also the probable long-term significance of events."[34] The top two events were the following:

> 1. **The new church**. The formation of the ELCA took place, according to Secretary Lowell Almen, "at 12:01 a.m. Central Daylight time Jan. 1 when the predecessor church corporations dissolved into the ELCA corporation." Some church leaders had gotten a head start on the new year: ELCA Bishop Herbert Chilstrom and more than half of the 65 synod bishops were installed before Jan. 1. Some 400 staffers began work at the new Chicago church-wide offices. Most U.S. newspapers, having given prior extensive coverage to the merger, took little note of the official start-up.
> 2. **Gay Seminarians**. The public announcement by three seminarians at Pacific Lutheran Seminary, Berkeley, Calif., that they were "openly gay" led to a crisis over the ordination of practicing homosexuals. The students had been certified for ordination by committees of predecessor church bodies. But subsequent action by ELCA bishops and "interim guidelines"

---

32. *Vision and Expectations: Ordained Ministers in the Evangelical Lutheran Church in America* (Chicago: The Evangelical Lutheran Church in America, 1990), 1.

33. *The Lutheran* is the main periodical of the ELCA, and receives its mandate from the ELCA's constitution to be published by the church through its publishing house. It receives wide readership, as most of the roughly 11,000 congregations receive multiple subscriptions, many paying for a copy per member of the congregation.

34. "Top Stories of the Year," *The Lutheran*, 4 January 1989, 22.

> adopted by the board of the Division for Ministry made it clear that ordination and pastoral calls would not be an option for gay men and lesbians--unless they committed themselves to celibacy.

The fact that news story number two ("Gay Seminarians") occurred at the same time (January 1988) as news story number one ("The New Church") drove the nature of the conflict. For this, a brief background may help to unpack the history and significance of the merger which formed the ELCA, thus making more clear the ethos surrounding the official beginning of the new church in January 1988, when the "crisis over practicing homosexuals" began.

The Lutheran Churches in the United States of America are all free associations formed by mostly northern European ethnic groups (e.g. Swedish, Danish, Norwegian, Slovak, German, Latvian, Hungarian, etc.) emigrating from the seventeenth through the nineteenth centuries. Many of the mother churches in Europe were state churches (e.g.. Sweden, Norway and Germany) and had confessional traditions which centered in the Lutheran reformation in sixteenth century Germany. Over time, these many immigrant Lutheran churches in the United States began to band together, often for purposes of sharing resources in social service and missionary work. Resulting cooperation often lead to discussion of and action on uniting church structures, and eventually the process narrowed the field down to, in the 1980s, three major groups of Lutherans in the United States.[35] In the late 1970s these three cooperated on the formation and printing of a joint hymnal, and although one of them pulled out at the end, for the groups remaining the process moved toward a vision of a final uniting merger bringing roughly two-thirds of all U. S. Lutherans together in one ecclesiastical body.

In 1982, a seventy-member Commission for a New Lutheran Church (CNLC) was formed with the task of working out the basis and practical steps by which the LCA, ALC, and AELC (see note 2) could consider merger. After four years, CNLC finished its work and voted 65-2 in favor of recommending their proposals, including a

35. This history is well told--Cf. Abdel Ross Wentz, *A Basic History of Lutheranism in America* (Philadelphia: Fortress Press, 1955). More recently published is the multi-author work, E. Clifford Nelson, ed. *The Lutherans in North America*, 2nd ed. (Philadelphia: Fortress, 1980).

constitution, bylaws, and other documents as well as a site for a new national headquarters and a name for the new church. The three bodies accepted the proposals at each of their national conventions and the plans began to be implemented. This brief history of mergers has a theological undergirding rooted in the confession of belief in "one holy catholic and apostolic church" in the Niceno-Constantinoplian creed[36] and the prayer of Jesus that all his followers "may be one" (John 17.22). These theological themes, as important as they are, only describe a motivation and public rhetoric for merger and unity; many changes in institutional practice were employed to overcome the practical difficulty of creating a working voluntary association between millions of people scattered across the United States. The choice of headquarters near Chicago's O'Hare airport is not surprising; the words of one leader in the merger process echo many in favoring "a single headquarters location as a symbol of unity."[37] Not surprisingly, the name chosen for the new headquarters reflects this desire to create unity: The Lutheran Center. After a tumultuous two years, the first Church Wide Assembly[38] met under the optimistic theme, "Many Voices, One Song."

Although each church shared a common set of historical and theological foundations in the Reformation, each had different contemporary structures and processes to bring to the merger. This meant, among other things, that change brought new networks of relations between different offices (bishops, pastors, theologians, officials) and different processes (candidacy, missions, social service,

---

36. This credal expression of Christianity is the most widely accepted confessional formulation, used both in various eastern traditions as well as by the Roman Catholic and Reformation churches of the West. Although most of the creed was written and approved at the Council of Nicea (or the First Ecumenical Council), 325 C.E., the section quoted comes from the final section written and approved at the Council of Constantinople (or the Second Ecumenical Council), 381 C.E.

37. Dr. Elwyn Ewald, speaking for the AELC Board of Directors, in the discussion over location of the new headquarters. Quoted in Edgar R. Trexler, "CNLC Satisfies Most LCA Merger Issues," *The Lutheran*, July 1986, 18.

38. The Church Wide Assembly is a biennial meeting of all constituencies in the church and the official policy making body within the church.

education). Like all processes and policies, the candidacy processes of the predecessor churches had to be streamlined into one process for the ELCA. Lutheran theologian and current President of Pacific Lutheran Theological Seminary Timothy F. Lull, reflecting on these events, characterized the candidacy processes of those Lutheran bodies which made up the ELCA. Though each had different processes, each was open to the ordination of sexually active gay and lesbian candidates if the activity was discrete--that is, done privately so as not to become an issue for the public life of the church. This was "not so much explicit policy as through a screening process that did not probe lives too deeply."[39] I cannot detail here all the specific differences and historical nuances between these three churches, but it is of paramount importance to recognize the sense of change and new direction underlying all aspects of the transition into the ELCA.[40]

The implementation of the new candidacy processes took place along with the official merger in January 1988. It was in the midst of the academic year, and thus in the midst of the final year of the processes for candidates across the eight seminaries of the church. Seniors were certified as prepared and ready to be called as pastor for a congregation after graduation by the predecessor bodies in the fall of 1987. It was in this larger context that in January 1988 Lutherans Concerned--a Lutheran ministry for lesbian and gay persons--announced in a news release that three "openly gay" seniors (Joel Workin, Jeff Johnson and James Lancaster) at Pacific Lutheran Theological Seminary (PLTS) had been certified for call and ordination. Shock waves roared through the church; the bishops of the western regions came to PLTS January 21-22 and discussed together with the faculty about precedents upon which to draw in dealing with the situation. The bishops issued a statement jointly with the faculty reaffirming "the current statement and practices of the Lutheran church that to be 'admittedly' homosexual in *orientation* does not in and of itself preclude ordination. The policy of

---

39. Timothy F. Lull, "Public and Private, Strong and Weak," *World and World*, 10 (Spring 1990): 141.

40. The editor of *The Lutheran*, Edgar R. Trexler, has written a book detailing the events of this history. See *Anatomy of a Merger* (Minneapolis: Augsburg, 1991).

the church is that practicing homosexuals will not be ordained [original emphasis]."[41]

At this early stage the "policy" was drawn from a mix of documents originally intended to speak to many different situations and drew only on the sections which explicitly dealt with homosexuality in relation to the traditional Lutheran grounding for theology of marriage: the order or design of creation. First, the policy drew on a section out of the 1970 LCA statement, *Sex, Marriage, and Family*, from the section titled "Some Current Issues," and used the following sentences: "Scientific research has not been able to provide conclusive evidence regarding the causes of homosexuality. Nevertheless, homosexuality is viewed biblically as a departure from the heterosexual structure of God's creation."[42] Second, the policy was built from the 1980 ALC statement *Human Sexuality and Sexual Behavior*, quoting from the section entitled "Considering Homosexuality." It focused on the following sentences: "We believe it appropriate to distinguish between homosexual orientation and homosexual behavior. Persons who do not practice their homosexual erotic preference do not violate our understanding of Christian sexual behavior. This Church regards the practice of homosexual acts as contrary to God's intent for his children. It rejects the contention that homosexual behavior is simply another form of sexual behavior equally valid with a dominant male/female pattern."[43] The policy drew secondarily from a 1982 memorandum from LCA bishop James R. Crumley Jr., and various ordination services calling pastors to "holy living." In short, no existing document spoke directly to the issue of sexuality and ordination and no practice was in place to question the candidates regarding their obedience.

Gary Pence, acting PLTS president at the time, commented that the seminary had followed "the *general guidelines or accepted positions* of the former ALC and LCA . . . (which) essentially *seemed to say* that homosexual orientation in and of itself does not bar a person from ordination, and that it is the practice of homosexuality that *could*

41. Jean Caffey Lyles, "Western Bishops Back Action on Gays," in *The Lutheran,* 16 March 1988, 23.

42. "ALC and LCA Precedents," in *The Lutheran,* 16 March 1988, 23.

43. Ibid.

constitute a bar to ordination [my emphasis]."[44] Students who, having admitted their homosexuality to a faculty member and who continued in seminary after hearing the church's views were assumed to be "prepared to comply."[45] *The Lutheran* editor Edgar Trexler echoes this ambiguity. "It is unclear if the certifying committees asked these seminarians whether they are 'practicing' homosexuals . . . . The assumption is that these gay seminarians, if ordained, will abide by the church's guidelines that pastors will be celibate if single and faithful if married."[46] It is ironic to note that the church did not and still does not recognize same-sex marriages, leaving one to ponder how the church's guidelines could be followed by gay seminarians. This irony only highlights the general character of the unfolding story: ambiguity, assumptions, and accepted positions which seem to say something and could constitute a rule. The rules were somewhat fluid, and that was perceived to be exactly the danger. A modern bureaucracy requires clarity on the level of formal reasons in order to carry out its more practical ends efficiently and effectively.

Recalling Weber's point that "calculable rules" are "of paramount importance"[47] for proper management, it comes as no surprise that church leaders were worried by their lack of clear policy and a process to implement it. As one example of this worry, *The Lutheran* magazine editor Edgar Trexler wrote, "We may never publish a more high-voltage news story than the one on pages 23 and 24. The news of certification of three openly gay seminarians for ordination cannot be avoided, even if the Evangelical Lutheran Church is not ready for it." Trexler reflects both "the explosiveness of this issue" and the fact that in terms of the bureaucracy's ability to respond, "its timing is awful."[48]

Another example, this time from the ELCA's 66 bishops meeting in mid-March 1988, amounts to censorship of the church's journal, *The Lutheran.* The bishops, after gaining access to the unpublished copies of two articles through the editor, privately persuaded the authors--who were the presiding bishops of, respectively, the Lutheran Church in

---

44. Lyles, "Western Bishops Back Action on Gays," 24.

45. Ibid.

46. Edgar R. Trexler, "The Issue of Ordaining Gays," in *The Lutheran*, 16 March 1988, 50.

47. Weber, "Bureaucracy," 215.

48. Trexler, "Ordaining Gays," 50.

America, James R. Crumley, Jr., and the American Lutheran Church, David W. Preus--to withdraw "opinion pieces [which] questioned the way former LCA and ALC statements and procedures were used in certification of the gay seminarians."[49] Paul Werger, Chairman of the Conference of Bishops, stated that "there was some confusion about their views and some seemed inaccurate. It seemed that they might further complicate the issue. We wanted to speak clearly, to bite the bullet, and suspend further discussion until the church has a chance to make up its mind."[50] The bishops did speak clearly, however, and could not delay in making a statement for as Werger said, "the issue had a lot of press."[51] Public opinion must have influenced the direction of the discussion--especially the responses of the membership--because of the connection between public image and ability to command the financial giving which sustains the church.[52]

The Conference of Bishops approved a statement that, according to ELCA Bishop Herbert W. Chilstrom, "affirms what has been the pattern in the three church bodies that formed the ELCA."[53] The

---

49. "Bishops' 'Intervention' Questioned," in *The Lutheran,* 11 May 1988, 26.

50. "Bishops: Gay Clergy Must Be Celibate," *The Lutheran*, 30 March 1988, 24.

51. Ibid.

52. This is an example of a letter that might be considered representative of the public opinion among the church membership which caused stress for the bishops and administrators. The letter is from Margaret Primmer, Logan, Ohio:

> For over 50 years I have supported our Lord's work through the Lutheran Church. I have always been proud to say, "I am a Lutheran." I cannot tell you the embarrassment, the pain and the anguish I felt when I read the news story about certifying gay seminarians. Pacific Lutheran Seminary faculty and Western Bishops wake up--get back to the Bible and Lutheran teaching!

in *The Lutheran*, 20 April 1988, 48. The importance of public opinion in driving the church in a more rule-oriented, conservative direction cannot be underestimated. Of the 21,000 lay member responses received to *The Church and Human Sexuality: A Lutheran Perspective*--a first draft statement on sexuality which suggested consideration of the full acceptance of gays--more than 65 percent rejected the draft and offered no positive comment. See "Background Material," in *Human Sexuality: A Working Draft*, 37.

53. "Bishops: Gay Clergy Must Be Celibate," 24.

statement echoes the views of the Western region bishops who met at PLTS in late January: homosexual orientation does not preclude ordination but homosexual practice does. A few days later, on March 20, Chilstrom sent a "pastoral letter" to all congregations in the ELCA reaffirming the statement approved by the Conference of Bishops. At the spring meeting of the Church Council, the permanent governance board for the ELCA, secretary of the church Lowell Almen spoke, warning them that "[t]he size of the new Evangelical Lutheran Church in America makes it 'highly visible' and 'horribly vulnerable' to the 'symbolic acts' of small groups." He referred directly to the "three young men from Berkeley" in his comments, saying that the impact of headlines leave lasting impressions in reader's minds. He urged the officials "to cooperate in shaping 'a clear, sharply defined identity' for the new church."[54] In Weber's words, "diplomacy [by which Weber means the public relations work of the purveyors of institutional identity] can only be publicly controlled to a very limited extent."[55] The need for institutional clarity in identity drove the efforts to clarify, in turn, the identity of the leadership and the possible public identities for those candidates who have been "certified" for ordination.

It follows from this drive toward purification of institutional and individual identity that by June 1988, all three of the seminarians at Berkeley--although all graduated in fine standing and with the certification of their former churches--had been removed from the active list of candidates. This action was taken because their "answers to celibacy questions were judged to lack 'sufficient clarity'." They were to "remain on a candidate list and under a bishop's care for one year."[56] The "special examination" of the three seminarians' intentions regarding sexual behavior and their subsequent removal from active participation in the placement process marks the beginning of the bureaucracy's search for solutions to the specific form of the problem in the process of candidacy.

The incident involving the three seminarians challenged the ecclesiastical authority of the ELCA beyond what could have been

54. "Almen: ELCA is Visible, Vulnerable," in *The Lutheran,* 1 June 1988, 24.

55. Weber, "Bureaucracy," 233.

56. "Two Gays Ruled Out as Candidates," in *The Lutheran*, 11 May 1988, 27.

expected. The issues raised did not have clear precedent in policy and process. One bishop from California sums up the perspective of many in leadership during this time: "The controversy over the gay candidates has complicated my life and consumed an enormous amount of energy."[57] Ironically, the challenge to church policy worked to strengthen the dehumanizing bureaucratic process. While the publication of the news that three gay candidates had passed through the approval process for ordained ministry was intended to publicize the fact that some "qualified" candidates were gay, instead the church authorities used this information to support reforming the processes that "qualified" candidates. Whatever the three candidates hoped the effects might be for gays and lesbians in the church, the response on the part of the institution has been a calculating and uncompromising imposition of an essentialized and bifurcated identity--be "homosexual" and remain a (celibate) candidate or do "homosexual practice" and face rejection.

With this explication of the history of the specific forms of the problem, I turn now to the history of the specific forms of the solutions as the institution efficiently and effectively re-formed itself in order to police the candidacy process more carefully.

History of the Solutions: Authority, Bureaucracy and Discipline

As early as April 1988, the Division for Ministry--among other things responsible for "developing programs for the recruitment, preparation and evaluation of candidates"[58]--began work on one specific revision of the candidacy processes in response to the crisis. In the beginning of the movement toward "calculable rules," *The Lutheran* reported:

> The ELCA may have to begin asking all candidates for ordination more explicit questions about their views on sexuality, according to an official at the ELCA Division for Ministry. The Rev. Craig

57. Ibid. The bishop quoted is Robert Miller, Pacifica Synod, Southern California.

58. Evangelical Lutheran Church in America, *Constitutions, Bylaws and Continuing Resolutions, Third revised edition* (Chicago: ELCA, 1993), 105.

> Settlage, director of candidacy, said that is one probable result of the uproar over 'openly gay' ministry candidates . . . . The candidacy director said issues raised by three gay seminarians have forced the church 'to look very thoughtfully at the whole issue of sexual conduct, and I think we will do that.' Homosexual candidates should not be subjected to a 'double standard' that treats heterosexuals more leniently, Settlage said. 'Now both will be asked for their understanding of the appropriate conduct.'[59]

This development curiously mirrors the general direction Weber predicted for modern bureaucratic operations: he claims that when one hears a cry for the introduction of regular training and "special examinations" one must not look for a suddenly awakened need for education as the purpose, but rather "the desire for restricting the supply for these positions."[60] But this would only explain the focus on suspected gay and lesbian candidates--those whom the church wants to restrict. Rev. Settlage's comments about extending the rule to all candidates simply highlights the way rationalizing takes on a life of its own, following the rule out to its own logical conclusions.

The first version of a rule, "Expectations Concerning Sexual Conduct of Candidates," developed by the Division for Ministry, became the groundwork upon which *Vision and Expectations* was built. The document begins with a quote from the Lutheran rite of ordination calling the person to lead the people of God "by your own example in faithful service and holy living." The document goes on to assert that "the issue of sexual conduct is an important one for candidates." "There are expectations" and "[i]t is important that there be a clear understanding of these expectations by all those involved in the candidacy process." Included in the document are two interim guidelines. Guideline one sets out the norm: "The appropriate setting for sexual intercourse and other erotic expressions of sexual intimacy is marriage." Guideline two spells out the implications of number one for gay candidates: "A pattern of behavior that includes homosexual erotic activity is conduct that is inappropriate and is reason for a person to be removed from candidacy in the ELCA." A last paragraph outlines the use of the guidelines in the candidacy process; they are to be used

---

59. "Why Not Quiz All the Candidates?," in *The Lutheran*, 11 May 1988, 27.

60. Weber, "Bureaucracy," 241.

by candidacy committees "to ascertain that every person seeking candidacy is aware of the expectations of this church concerning sexual conduct" and to "ask every person if he or she is committed to live a life that is consistent with those expectations."[61]

The guidelines were requested by Bishop Chilstrom and constituted a large part of the work of the Division for Ministry in its first two years. In its first biennial report, the Division defined its work in terms "as broad as undergirding the ministry of all the baptized members of the church, and as specific as providing guidance to committees that select candidates for ordained . . . service." The report continues under the heading Roster Standards and Policies: "The maintenance of the official ELCA roster involves the establishment of standards and expectations for rostered persons....[t]he first such policy to be developed related to the ordination of homosexual persons. It was written after candidates, who had been approved by the predecessor churches, openly announced themselves to be homosexual."[62] The interim guidelines served for nearly two years as the church worked to formulate and implement new standards and practices which more closely regulated the process by which candidates come into the ministry.

Finally in the fall of 1990, *Vision and Expectations* was released. It begins with an open letter from Bishop Chilstrom to the whole church followed by an introduction which rehearses the constitutional vision for ordained ministers. The rest of the document is divided into four sections, each section headed by a question from the ordination service; the sections are 1) The Call To Ordained Ministry, 2) Faithfulness to the Church's Confession, 3) The Ordained Minister as Person and Example and 4) Faithful Witness. Under section three, the "normative" sexual ethics is reinscribed:

> *Sexual conduct.* The expectations of this church regarding the sexual conduct of its ordained ministers are grounded in the understanding that human sexuality is a gift of God and that ordained ministers are to live in such a way as to honor this gift . . . . Single ordained ministers are expected to live a chaste life. Married ordained ministers are expected to live in fidelity to their

---

61. "Expectations Concerning Sexual Conduct," 2.

62. Evangelical Lutheran Church in America, *1989 Church Wide Assembly Reports and Records*, 87-8.

> spouses, giving expression to sexual intimacy within a marriage relationship that is mutual, chaste and faithful. Ordained ministers who are homosexual in their self-understanding are expected to abstain from homosexual sexual relationships.[63]

These few sentences constitute the central idea--the normative view of acceptable sexual expression--driving the creation of the entire document.

The normative view of marriage is even more strongly present in the "officially" disciplinary document, *Definitions and Guidelines for Discipline*, in its section for discipline of ordained ministers. It says the following: "The biblical understanding which this church affirms is that the normative setting for sexual intercourse is marriage. In keeping with this understanding, chastity before marriage and fidelity within marriage are the norm . . . . Practicing homosexual persons are precluded from the ordained ministry of this church." It is worth noting that the original edition of *Definitions and Guidelines for Discipline* included in the *Reports and Records* adds one sentence to the beginning of what I quote above; "Sexuality is a gift from God to all persons."[64] It is not surprising that this sentence proved too dangerous for inclusion in the final, public version, not because of sexuality's gift status, but because it is a gift *to all.* The language of sexuality as a gift offered the various writers of *Vision and Expectations* a strategic advantage in their efforts: sexuality as "gift" makes it an object, an external possession to be used properly --if you want to be ordained.[65]

In its 1991 report to the Churchwide Assembly, The Division for Ministry described *Vision and Expectations* process of construction:

> The Division for Ministry also developed a draft document describing the gifts and abilities needed by this church in those who serve as ordained ministers. A broad consultation process that extended for one year--involving the division board, the Conference of Bishops, synods, seminaries, and synodical

---

63. *Vision and Expectations*, 13.

64. Evangelical Lutheran Church in America, *1989 Church Wide Assembly Reports and Records, Vol. II* (Chicago, Office of the Secretary, 1990), 547.

65. For a critique of sexuality as "gift" see Martha E. Stortz, "Human Sexuality and the Christian Faith," *dialog* 32 (Winter 1993): 62-65.

> candidacy committees--led to the development of the final document entitled, "Vision and Expectations: Ordained Ministers in the Evangelical Lutheran Church in America."[66]

Drafted by the Division for Ministry, the document was distributed to all ELCA congregations, pastors and seminaries with a cover letter from Bishop Chilstrom.[67] This model of policy creation makes crystal clear Foucault's point that disciplinary power is anonymous power--"for although surveillance rests on individuals, its functioning is that of a network of relations from top to bottom, but also from bottom to top and laterally . . . ." Thus no single individual bears authority or responsibility for the effects of this sort of power--no one person can hold or wield "the uninterrupted play of calculated gazes" upon which disciplinary power depends for its reality and effectiveness.[68] *Vision and Expectations* embodies these calculated gazes which continuously assert their hold over the candidates.

It comes as no surprise that great care was taken in the production of the document--much was at stake in its development. The top two stories of 1989 are a commentary on the stakes:

> 1. **A $15 million deficit** forced staff layoffs, hiring and salary freezes and other cost-cutting measures by ELCA church wide units. Although giving by church members rose, congregations and synods kept a sizable proportion of funds at home, sending less than projected to churchwide offices in Chicago.
> 2. **Challenging church policy**, two San Francisco congregations called openly homosexual seminary graduates as assistant pastors.[69]

The ordinations took place January 20, 1990, in St. Paulus Lutheran Church with over 900 supporters and 42 ordained ELCA clergy participating. According to a report in *The Lutheran,* a "statement from

---

66. See Evangelical Lutheran Church in America, *1991 Church Wide Assembly Reports and Records, Vol. I* (Chicago: Office of the Secretary, 1992), 130.

67. "It's Official: What ELCA Asks of Clergy," in *The Lutheran*, 28 November 1990, 23.

68. Michel Foucault, *Discipline and Punish,* 176.

69. "Lutheran Headlines of '89," in *The Lutheran*, 3 January 1990, 24.

Bishop Chilstrom's office called the rule-breaking by the two churches 'unacceptable and regrettable'." After reiterating that the three irregular ordinations were not recognized by the ELCA, "the statement said uniform ordination standards must prevail 'for the integrity and unity of this church'."[70] The issues of sexuality and ordination were placing a great challenge to the authority of the ELCA, as the bishops said, "we are deeply distressed over the challenge to the unity of this church."[71] Bishop Chilstrom was quoted in informal discussion as saying, "If I only read my mail, I'd jump out a window . . . ."[72] Surely many other factors have played a part in the gravity of the situation. Still, the fact that "nothing troubled the new church's undertakings as much as the failure of financing"[73] had effects on how the officials viewed the challenges and worked out responses to them.

Directly connected to the sexuality issues, the unity and authority of the church was being challenged fiscally. In a meeting with the Church Council,[74] Bishop Chilstrom acknowledged that the deficit was "critical," and gave several reasons for it. The first and most loaded, given the larger context of the statement, was the following: "Merger upsets longstanding loyalties. Time is required to build new ones." In response to the deficit, The Office of Finance report at the same Church Council meeting made it clear that more than time would be required to build new loyalties. They called for "an ongoing process to review the structure of the church and to make periodic recommendations . . . for revisions that will improve the ability of the church to most effectively, efficiently and economically respond to the needs of the church."[75] *Vision and Expectations* and the documents which preceded

---

70. Jean Caffey Lyles, "Panel Suspends 2 S.F. Congregations," in *The Lutheran*, 8 August 1990, 29.

71. "Text of bishops' statement," in *The Lutheran,* 11 April 1990, 24.

72. Edgar R. Trexler, "Bishops: Gay Ordinations Threaten Unity," in *The Lutheran*, 11 April 1990, 24.

73. Trexler, *Anatomy of a Merger*, 251.

74. The Church Council is a 36 member committee elected in national assembly for policy making and on-going management of church life in between biennial Church Wide Assemblies. Also active are two youth advisors and nine advisory bishops.

75. "Church Council OKs Mission 90," in *The Lutheran*, 24 May 1989, 21-22. The language here recalls Weber: "The decisive reason for the advance of bureaucratic organization has always been its purely technical

it constitute such re-forming efforts at efficiency and technical superiority; such "calculable rules" governing the life of the church are central to the establishment of authority. In the heat of debate over the construction of this series of documents, Bishop "Chilstrom told the [Church] Council that the church faces an 'emergency situation' in which it needs a stated position on the ordination of homosexuals. 'The documents of the predecessor churches and the statement of the Conference of Bishops do not hold a lot of water now. After two years, people want someone in authority in this church to say something'."[76]

Guidance and Necessary Evaluation: Candidacy Processes and the Interview

Developing Candidacy Process

The marked continuity from early "Interim Guidelines for Candidacy (1987)" to the "Candidacy Manual (1989)" and the second edition revised "Candidacy Manual (1994)" shows that the basic rationality behind the process of candidacy was present from the inception of the ELCA. As noted above, the introduction of a "special examination" about sexuality during candidacy interviews has been at the heart of developing documents--including *Vision and Expectations*--which have allowed direct questioning of familiarity with the church's position without "inappropriate" questions about personal life.[77] Under the guise of respectability, the committee members don't ask; the documents carry the questions by which the candidates question and shape themselves. *Vision and Expectations* itself takes on the disciplinary role of inquisitor. In this section, I first offer a brief summary of the Division for Ministry rhetoric around implementation of the process--

superiority."Cf. "Bureaucracy," 214.

76. Jean Caffey Lyles, "Discipline Policy: Too Legalistic?," in *The Lutheran,* 20 December 1989, 22.

77. The document "Expectations Concerning Sexual Conduct of Candidates" includes an assurance that although committees are to evaluate candidates, committees will not "be requesting candidates to share personal and intimate aspects of their lives. Such inquires are themselves inappropriate. It is rather the responsibility of the candidacy committees to ascertain that every person seeking candidacy is aware of the expectations of this church concerning sexual conduct, and to ask every person if he or she is committed to live a life that is consistent with those expectations."

the work of implementation requires more attention to developments in the process, especially regarding the use of *Vision and Expectations*. Then, I will turn my attention to how the basic candidacy process works as a set of examinations "making" candidates acceptable or not, remembering Foucault's work on correct training and the use of examinations as tools for analysis.

From the beginning the Division for Ministry has spent much time and energy working on issues of candidacy. Every two years a major report is made by the Division to the Church Wide Assembly and is printed in the *Reports and Records*. Each of the three reports to date makes plain what amount of energy and time has been spent in the area of candidacy--only one of many areas of responsibility for the Division. According to the 1989 report, the first since the beginning of the church, "the initial major effort was to develop operational procedures that would enable the ELCA candidacy process to provide for the guidance and necessary evaluation of some 325 graduating students preparing for ordained and associate in ministry positions in the new church." Drafts of a "Manual on Candidacy" were worked out from the "Interim Guidelines for Candidacy," training sessions were held around the country for candidacy committee members and the first official evaluations were carried out. A first policy was developed ("Expectations Concerning Sexual Conduct of Candidates") and implemented in the process of guidance and evaluation.[78]

By the second report at the 1991 Church Wide Assembly, candidacy committees were organized in all sections of the church. "Patterns for interviewing and testing candidates for ordination were put in place . . . [and] candidacy efforts included regional consultations and training of candidacy committee chairpersons, interview training for committee members, and the development of a revised *Candidacy Manual*."[79] As is said above, *Vision and Expectations* came about and was approved for distribution to all pastors, congregations and seminaries. Two years later, the practice of representing the process had become almost wholly positive, no longer responding to crisis but working to ensure that authority and order reigned throughout the church. In the 1993 Church

78. Division for Ministry, *1989 Church Wide Assembly Reports and Records, Vol I*, 87.

79. Division for Ministry, *1991 Church Wide Assembly Reports and Records, Vol. I*, 121.

Wide Assembly report, the first item under the Division for Ministry's self-description was the following:

> In order for faithful ministry to occur in congregations, there must be a steady supply of carefully selected, well educated, and approved new leaders to serve as pastors and associates in ministry. Candidacy committees in each synod of the Evangelical Lutheran Church in America work carefully with each of the 1,400 candidates preparing for service as rostered leaders in this church.[80]

This calm report belies the frantic nature with which the Division created a process allowing careful observation of the whole group of candidates in order to "carefully" select the appropriate new leaders.

Foucault's work on pastoral power and its focus on a watchful gaze on the whole flock as individual sheep emphasizes the way in which candidacy committees are pastoral vis à vis the candidates under their care. According to the 1993 report, this individual care for candidates is carried out through a "strong network of ELCA candidacy committees working with each synod, which interview, evaluate, consult with, and counsel each person preparing for a church occupation." It was noted that "the division conducted an extensive review of the candidacy process . . . [and] some adjustments were made in the candidacy process to make it more streamlined and effective."[81] As the process reaches mature form, direct reference to sexuality fades from the picture. As the basis, buried in the documents and process themselves, this regulation of sexuality becomes a "natural" fixture on the landscape of the candidacy process.

The Examinations

The process now centers around three examinations of the individual candidate by his/her candidacy committee. These three examinations are the sites in which the candidacy committees carry out their mandate; the candidacy committee "oversees the care of the candidate and . . .

---

80. Division for Ministry, *1993 Church Wide Assembly Reports and Records, Vol I* (Chicago: Evangelical Lutheran Church in America, 1994), 67.

81. Ibid.

provides the guidance and supervision of those seeking to serve."[82] The first examination takes place after the candidate has read and utilized the ELCA discernment resource *What Shall I Say? Discerning God's Call to Ministry*, after a congregation has filed a "Congregation Registration of a Person Seeking Candidacy" form with the appropriate candidacy committee, after filing an "Application for Entrance to Candidacy in the Evangelical Lutheran Church in America" form with the candidacy committee, after an initial interview with a person trained in the "Initial Interview Training Workshop" and the filing of the "Initial Interviewer's report" with the candidacy committee, and finally, after a psychological evaluation and the filing of the "Psychological Evaluation and Career Consultation" form with the candidacy committee. With this information, the candidacy committee evaluates the candidate and makes an entrance decision. The focus in this first examination centers on correct speech--"What Shall I Say?" is indeed the question. A positive decision qualifies one for a packet of information on the various seminaries of the ELCA along with candidacy information including *Vision and Expectations*. This allows the process of self-examination to begin; candidates are not explicitly questioned about adherence to the expectations until the final examination. With this first process complete, one is able to apply for and, if offered, accept admission to a seminary.

The second examination should take place after the first year of the seminary curriculum and is a time when "an individual's progress in formation for ministry may be assessed, as well as a time to review developmental issues identified earlier in the entrance process."[83] The central focus is the candidate's preparation of "The Endorsement Essay" and subsequent questioning by the candidacy committee in an "Endorsement Interview" following a model interview found in the *Candidacy Manual*.[84] The process here focuses on "correct" writing about oneself, explaining the progress made toward a correct representation of self which can be "endorsed" by the church as close to the norm. Relevant materials include the candidate's file from the entrance process, "current seminary transcripts, the entrance decision

82. ELCA, *Candidacy Manual* (Chicago: Division for Ministry, 1994), 8.

83. Ibid.,157.

84. Ibid., 165-166.

report and the Endorsement Essay."[85] Possible outcomes include endorsement, postponement, and denial, followed by the filing of the appropriate "Endorsement Decision for Candidacy in the Evangelical Lutheran Church in America" form with the Division for Ministry.

The third examination should take place in the last year of the seminary curriculum. The candidacy committee will consider whether to give "approval" to each candidate. This decision, according to the *Candidacy Manual*, "is one of the most important decisions made in the life of the Church."[86] Therefore, it comes as no surprise that the "purpose of the Approval interview is to review and inquire in depth into the candidate's readiness."[87] The approval decision is made on the basis of all previous materials, updated transcripts, written reports from fieldwork supervisors, a faculty interview, recommendation, and evaluative report (Form D), along with a set of "Approval Essays" written and submitted to the Candidacy Committee. The "Approval Interview" is carried out according to a model from the *Candidacy Manual*, and its contents are based largely on the four basic sections of *Vision and Expectations*. The possible outcomes of the interview are three: approval, postponement, and denial.

An approval interview, according to the *Candidacy Manual* "Approval Interview Guide,"[88] would be something like the following: an approval essay is written to answer basic theological and pastoral questions which are explicitly formulated on the basis of *Vision and Expectations*. The two documents which provide the basis for approval decisions are the Constitutions, Bylaws, and Continuing Resolutions of the ELCA and *Vision and Expectations*. In theory, then, the committee would know well both of these documents, would have read the candidate's approval essays and have reviewed the file for other reports and information on the candidates career. One person, called a "relator," should have maintained a relationship with the student during the entire candidacy process and should now "identify prime topics to cover during the interview and identify persons who will ask lead questions."[89]

---

85. Ibid.
86. Ibid., 185.
87. Ibid.
88. Ibid., 186-188.
89. Ibid., 186.

The interview should have five parts. First, under the heading "Introductions and Welcome," the Guide suggests there is "understandably a considerable anxiety for candidates as they prepare for this interview. It is useful to make certain that the candidates understand the purpose of this interview."[90] Becoming "approved" depends on "correct" speech and writing, according to the years of training and self-examination. Second, questions are asked regarding the specific contents of the candidates' answers to the approval essay. This is followed by a third section focused on other reports and issues raised by the "relator" in the preparation for the interview. Fourth, the committee is to ask "Questions related to *Vision and Expectations*," especially in order to examine "the candidate's knowledge of and commitment to the expectations of the ELCA."[91] Six suggested questions are listed which cover the four main sections of the document. The last question comes to the point: "Is it your intention to seek to fulfill these expectations in your ministry?"[92]

The moment of truth has come; the years of work creating the candidacy process and the years of work this individual has undertaken have produced the three effects of examination. An objectified individual quite open to the committee's vision (surveillance) now exists, at least to the extent that the process has elicited (self-) representations throughout its various stages. On the basis of these (self-) representations, reports, essays, etc. the candidate is "knowable" and open to comparison to the expectations (the Norm). Therefore, the candidate can be made a "case" and is given an individuality on the basis of the process of answering the question, "Is it your intention to seek to fulfill these expectations in your ministry?" As Foucault said, "power produces; it produces reality; it produces domains of objects and rituals of truth. The individual and the knowledge that may be gained of him belong to this production."[93] The interview ends by telling the candidate how and when to expect the decision.

In this chapter, I have shown how the developing structures for training pastoral leadership in the ELCA have been driven by particular events related to sexuality and authority. Specifically, a set of

90. Ibid., 187.
91. Ibid.
92. Ibid., 188.
93. Foucault, *Discipline and Punish,* 194.

examinations, centering on documents which outline the rules of "acceptable" sexual behavior, have been institutionalized in order to regularize the population of the clergy and to "make" candidates in the image of these expectations. I have used the development of the document, *Vision and Expectations*, and the development of its use, as a way to illumine how the church re-forms through the quintessentially modern techniques of bureaucracy. Application of these techniques in order to respond to the challenge to authority should result, some would argue, in the construction of a well-ordered leadership, and therefore a well-ordered church.

On the other hand, the discourses of the bureaucracy may offer means for sophisticated resistances to develop. In 1993, "The Extraordinary Candidacy Project" was launched by concerned Lutherans for the primary purpose of offering "support to ELCA candidates who have been denied ordination and to pastors who have been removed from the ministry solely because of their sexual orientation." The project includes "Extraordinary Candidacy Committees," and a "National Extraordinary Placement Committee" which "work to evaluate seminary students, graduates and pastors . . . helping match approved pastoral candidates with congregations and agencies that are willing to consider issuing a call."[94] The EEC even uses the *Vision and Expectations* document--minus the sentence regarding homosexual practice and celibacy--as a means of protest against the document's use in excluding gay and lesbian candidates from the process.

This response, however promising and courageous, focuses on the structure and processes of the institution. The argument underlying this entire book contends that work toward shifting the institutional structure and practices remains limited in power without a critical analysis of the current *theological* defense on the part of the bureaucracy in its uncompromising rejection of gay and lesbian people. The ELCA appropriated a certain part of the theological heritage of its predecessor bodies--namely an ahistorical interpretation of the "orders of creation"--thereby creating "calculable rules" linking God's intention for sexuality solely to male/female marriage. Rethinking marriage theology, then, and especially the ways in which current theology uses the resources of

94. From a brochure, "The Extraordinary Candidacy Project: A Call To Action," Berkeley, May 1994. See www.dnai.com/~bfalk/ecp.html.

the Lutheran tradition, becomes a foundational piece of work to be done before the ethical judgements and institutional policies will shift.

But, some might argue: what the ELCA has done represents not only the best they could do under difficult circumstances, but a theological and policy position in line with historic Lutheran positions on these issues. Such a person might think that what I argue are outrageous developments instead look like laudable efforts on the part of church leadership. Let me state clearly here: I do not accuse any single person nor do I especially focus on individual intent to harm others. Surely many complicated motivations and actions on the part of many people contributed to the current situation in the ELCA. If anything, my analysis in this chapter shows how haste, fear, and defensiveness do not make for thoughtful policy; even less do they make for good theology.

Furthermore, the church must think carefully about whether the process for candidacy it now uses actually gathers helpful information about candidates or, as Foucault helps to recognize, creates certain sorts of people. And if the process of candidacy, now fully based on a system of examinations, is a formative process, then the church needs to ask some very serious questions: how is the process forming candidates for ministry? What sort of formation would be desirable? Does the church want such formation to be centered on interrogation regarding sexual identity and behavior? And lastly, is such a theology of sexuality produced for the explicit purpose of excluding gay and lesbians from pastoral leadership our best theology of sexuality and marriage?

While I sincerely ask these questions to you, the reader, I nonetheless have strong views especially on the latter question. As I showed in the chapter above, the ELCA has drawn on the most rigid construal of an inherently conservative theological tradition. Further, the ELCA lifted theological arguments out of their various historical contexts, thus making it seem as if Lutherans have always spoken with one voice on this issue. Lastly, this theological retrieval has been deployed in an insidious way to harm and exclude those in our church who already experience great marginalization in our society. These moves made by the ELCA in dealing with the issue of candidacy, "homosexuality," and ordination, I argue, are worthy of moral outrage.

A two-fold effort can be undertaken by those outraged at this theological legitimation of the system of interrogation and exclusion embodied in the candidacy process and justified by "orders of creation" theology. This perspective, drawn from what I consider the best study officially adopted by U. S. Lutherans on sexuality, *Sex, Marriage, and the Family* (1970), suggests the following. The first step involves "a serious attempt to get at the fundamental concepts and relationships that lay behind earlier judgements."[95] The book up to this point has attempted this effort. As I turn to the last chapter, I take up the task of constructive work. Such a second step, *Sex, Marriage and the Family* suggests, requires taking with great seriousness that "aspects of human life can change so radically that specific ethical judgements must sometimes be turned upside down if their essential meaning is to be preserved."[96] Chapter five below works out some first steps down this important two-fold path toward more inclusive marriage theology and church policy.

---

95. *Sex, Marriage, and Family*, ed. Tilberg, 18.

96. Ibid. These two moves closely follow Luther himself, who always questioned the specific judgements made on the basis of love. "A law which goes against love is not a law; love is the mistress and the teacher of the law. She bids the law be silent in cases when following it without moderation might teach injustice instead of justice." Martin Luther, translated and quoted by Haile, "Algorithm and *Epikeia*," 508.

Chapter 5

Promises of Fidelity: An Inclusive Theology of Marriage

> The infusion of historical relativity into the orders can also break their linkage to an ethical conservatism that always finds it necessary to stand against every revolutionary development, thus denying the freedom of God to do a new thing or two in the world.
> Carl E. Braaten, "God in Public Life"

Can Lutherans build a theological and ethical position on marriage and sexuality that both fully welcomes lesbian and gay Christians and upholds the fundamental bases of church teachings on marriage and sexuality? After a long and careful argument showing how Lutherans in the main have used "orders of creation" theology as a defensive tool against unwelcome social change, it is clear I worry about those who would reject all that is new and unfamiliar. Nevertheless, I do not wish to swing to the other pole where traditional arguments are set aside as irrelevant. Rather, I argue in this chapter for a middle road position--indeed I argue that such an affirming yet traditional position is not only possible but deeply faithful exactly to those theological insights most fundamental in the historical materials.

The Letter and The Spirit

Constructive theological efforts would fail at the outset, however, if I were to turn to what Luther and twentieth century Lutheran statements said explicitly about homosexuality. Luther almost never mentioned same-sex relations; only once, commenting on the story of Sodom, did he explicitly respond to the issue. He wrote,

> Moses proceeds with a terrible sin. I for my part do not like dealing with this passage, because so far the ears of the Germans are innocent of and uncontaminated by this monstrous depravity; for even though this disgrace, like other sins, has crept in through an ungodly soldier and a lewd merchant, still the rest of the people are unaware of what is being done in secret.[1]

Clearly, an ethic for same-sex relationships goes nowhere with the "letter" of Luther's views.

A turn to the last forty years of United States Lutheran reflection in official statements offers little more help. The earliest statement that dealt explicitly with the issue was the ULCA statement, "Marriage and Family Life," written primarily by Harold Haas. The statement describes homosexuality as "one of the most common types of sexual deviation." Same-sex relations were seen as "a denial of God's intention in creation" and thus a denial of the "fundamental structure of creation."[2] While the ELCA has failed thus far to adopt an official statement on sexuality more broadly or homosexuality in particular, chapter four above makes clear how the ELCA produced an institutional practical theology by drawing on two statements of predecessor churches which describe homosexuality as "a departure from the heterosexual structure of God's creation" and "contrary to God's intent for his children."[3] As I show in chapters three and four, this language was central in official statements of Lutheran churches down to the present, seemingly leaving little room for a re-formed relational theology and ethics.

Theology and Policy: Reasons for Revision

Why reform the church's teaching? Why does the "letter" of the church's position not serve adequately? As I suggested at the

---

1. Luther, "Lectures on Genesis 15-20 (1535-1545)," 251-2.

2. "Marriage and Family Life," in ULCA, *Minutes of the twentieth Biennial Convention 1956*, 1137-1138.

3. *Sex, Marriage and Family*, 12; *Human Sexuality and Sexual Behavior*, 15.

conclusion to chapter four, the use of theology in the ELCA and its predecessor churches has at times been based on haste, fear, and defensiveness. When this was the case, the outcome has been dangerous policy and bad theology. The ELCA study guide and first statement on sexuality, published in 1991 and 1993 respectively, dealt creatively and constructively with a broad scope of issues (purposefully excluding the issue of ordination for gay and lesbian candidates for ministry). However, the official theology of sexuality (embodied in the documents *Vision and Expectations* and *Definitions and Guidelines for Discipline*) orientating the ELCA and its policies derives from a focus on what was explicitly said about homosexuality over the last forty years in U. S. Lutheran statements.

Before turning to the constructive section of this chapter, let me briefly sum up my response to a key question implicit thus far: What is so troublesome about such marriage theology undergirding the ELCA's candidacy and juridical documents, that is, about its institutional practical theology? I will argue that four things are problematic: its content, its form, its context of development, and its effects.

First, the problem with content. Marriage theology drawing on the "heterosexual order of creation" is rooted in a long tradition of arguments from biology. One finds this today, in Luther and other historical figures, and in biblical texts. Such an argument, buttressed by a certain reading of the first chapters of Genesis, focuses attention on the natural complementarity of male and female anatomy. This view leans heavily on procreation for legitimation; any sex act that violates this natural order of things is viewed as a transgression of God's intention in creation. As I show especially in chapter three, Lutherans have increasingly seen that sex is much more than procreation in the biological sense; it also is life-giving (pro-creative) in a personal, relational sense. Within a committed relationship, a healthy, mutually fulfilling sexual relationship can bring joy, closeness, and deepened commitment. Furthermore, a focus on the personal and relational aspects of sex offers a space for the church to hear the testimony of gay and lesbian Christians on their experience of joy and love in faithful committed relationships.

Second, the problem with form. As it has typically been employed, "orders of creation" theology has borne a timeless, 'divine fiat' sense as if God from the beginning of time decreed the modern norm of marriage as one man and one woman. Despite what Karl Haas and others have argued in the past, chapter three showed that Lutherans have increasingly seen that the form of marriage as an "order" of creation has changed throughout human history and across cultures. Even Luther could argue as much: in response to questions on marriage troubles in his own day, he argued

> We have to take into consideration the character and ways of our own land when we want to make or apply laws and rules, because our rules and laws are based on the character of our land and its ways and not on those of the land of Moses, just as Moses' laws are based on the ways and character of his people and not those of ours.[4]

Carl Braaten, in a careful exposition of "orders of creation" theology, notes a similar cord; historical relativity in the form of marriage is properly part of the "orders" theology.

Third, the problem with context of development. My argument in chapters three and four make clear that in almost every case, crises and threats of ecclesial chaos drove an atmosphere of ethical conservatism that searched through the tradition for a "rule" to prematurely end constructive (read: dangerous) debate. "Orders of creation" theology is intended as a way to talk about general structures of social life given by God as means to counteract the destructive work of the devil and serve in the preservation of the world. As such, the discernment of the relation between one of the three orders--the church, the household and its domestic economy, political government--and the particulars of one historical time and place constitutes a most serious task for the church. Indeed, Luther spoke of God working through a Christian's participation in the orders as God working "behind a mask." Often enough, a politically expedient use of "order of creation" theology seems to have taken place in times of crisis, a fact that should give the church pause given the German Lutheran use of this same technique to legitimate support for Hitler during World War II.[5]

---

4. Luther, "On Marriage Matters," Robert C. Schultz, trans. *LW* 46, 291.

5. See Werner Elert and Paul Althaus, *The Ansbach Proposal as a Response to the Barmen Theological Declaration*, in which they argue that in the political order one is subject to the orders and must obey, giving

Lastly, the problem of effects. As chapter four tries to make clear, "orders of creation" theology was taken out of context to formulate church policy. The intent, however nicely articulated in terms of the "high expectations this church has of its ordained ministry,"[6] nonetheless effected the marginalization and exclusion of an entire group of persons. It did so by refusing their calling by God to pastoral ministry unless they vow life-long celibacy. It did so by refusing to bless their committed relationships even though the church's tradition allows that by their promises of fidelity, they truly are married in the sight of God. And these negative effects hurt the whole church. The ELCA has lost vibrant and effective pastors and congregations. It now has a candidacy process literally centered on examination of sexual identity and behavior. And only slowly, here and there, are places made safe enough for gay and lesbian Christians among us to share their testimony; to share with the greater church their faithfulness--as Timothy Lull put it, "how they have not lost heart."[7]

Toward an Inclusive Theology of Marriage

The four troublesome aspects of current ELCA marriage theology suggest that Lutherans should not fall into the trap of simply retrieving the theological ideas of a previous generation for application in the present. Thus, the fact that Luther and recent Lutheran statements come to negative conclusions on homosexuality does not weigh as heavily as it may appear at first glance. The point is *not* to discover exactly which ethical prescriptions based on theological conclusions were applied to 1520 Germany or 1955 United States contexts. Rather, careful attention to the fundamental theological grounds and the *method* for deriving ethical prescriptions from those grounds bear most directly on work before today's Christians. Faithful action in response to the work of a living God requires new theological work based on a justified

---

thanks for the protection that they offer. On this basis they give thanks for and require obedience to the Fuhrer, Adolf Hitler. The document is found in Karl Hertz, ed., *Two Kingdoms and One World: A Sourcebook in Christian Social Ethics* (Minneapolis: Augsburg, 1976), 189-191.

6. Evangelical Lutheran Church in America, *Definition and Guidelines for Discipline*, 3.

6. Timothy F. Lull, "Learning from the Reformers," 61.

method and fundamental theological grounds in order to interpret what God is doing in the present.

An *inclusive* theology of marriage attempts to speak faithfully from a tradition of Christian thought to a contemporary experience. This perspective requires two related moves. First, careful and generous listening to the present is required in order to avoid hasty judgements against those who are different from me. On this count, I wish to preclude taking a theological idea of another age and using it without revision, especially in actions that negatively affect many persons. Second, serious attention to the wisdom of one's tradition is required in order to avoid mere relevance. Here, I wish to preclude taking wholesale the current mood of society as the most faithful response to the present. Following James Gustafson's methodological reflections (detailed in chapter one), I explicitly focus on 'experience' as the primary way Christians know God and God's world; yet experiences and the truths known from it are tested by the fundamental wisdom of Scripture and tradition (the testimony of experiences of God from the faithful over thousands of years). One caveat: as Luke Timothy Johnson has argued,

> nothing could be more offensive that to challenge tradition on the basis of casual or unexamined experience, as though God's revelation were obvious or easy, or reducible to popularity polls. The call to discernment of human experience is a call not to carelessness, but to its opposite; it is a call to the rigorous asceticism of attentiveness.[8]

It is the latter of these that I claim regarding the role of experience in theological work; such attentiveness marked Luther's work and the best of the U. S. Lutheran work on sexual ethics. I now turn to Luther in an effort to see how his efforts to revise the theology and ethics of sexuality and marriage during his lifetime might inform work today.

Luther

In chapter two, I developed an interpretation of Luther's mature views on sexuality and marriage by highlighting three related reversals wrought by his theology of sexuality and marriage. Luther reversed a

---

8. Luke Timothy Johnson, *Scripture and Discernment: Decision Making In The Church* (Nashville: Abingdon, 1996), 144.

tradition which: (1) devalued sex and marriage while uplifting celibacy; (2) made marriage a sacramental rather that civil affair; and (3) viewed the work of marriage as necessary but not properly Christian work. Reformation historian Kristen Kvam argues that the church today has the most to learn from Luther where his views were unconventional. She writes that "breaking with conventional modes of thinking requires effort and entails risk. Luther must think it important to counter traditional ways of thinking about sexuality, especially the traditions that uphold the propriety of celibacy vows and that minimize the significance of embodiment and sexual activity."[9] Kvam suggests, as I have above, that Luther's method and fundamental commitments are most helpful to the theological work of today.

Luther built both his criticisms of current ideals and practices and his new theological view on a two-fold attention to experiences gained in pastoral work and his study of scripture. One of Luther's first major public works, the "Address to the Christian Nobility of the German Nation," advocated drastic changes in many spheres of churchly life, including sexuality and marriage. Luther wrote this work not out of an interest in self-promotion nor mere academic debate but rather out of a priest's moral outrage over the situation of Christians "oppressed by distress and affliction."[10] Two years later, in the introduction to his treatise on "The Estate of Marriage," Luther comments that the current state of marriage "has given rise to so many dreadful abuses and false situations, that I would much prefer neither to look into the matter nor to hear of it. But timidity is no help in an emergency; I must proceed. I must try to instruct poor bewildered consciences, and take up the matter boldly."[11] These sorts of statements are everywhere in Luther's works leading the reader to keep in mind that Luther not only served as professor but also pastor. His experiences of the problems and his motivations for action were rooted in moral outrage, to be sure, but just as much by deep compassion for the plight of the people.

Luther's unconventional arguments against monastic vows and compulsory celibacy for all who wished to serve God aright can serve to both summarize Luther's method and the fundamental theological

---

9. Kristen E. Kvam, "'Honoring God's Handiwork': Challenges of Luther's Doctrine of Creation," in Lutz, ed. *A Reforming Church*, 183.

10. Luther, "To the Christian Nobility," 124-5.

11. Luther, "The Estate of Marriage," 17.

grounds upon which he built his constructive views. On the issue of priests and celibacy, Luther spoke from experience: "We also see how the priesthood has fallen, and how many a poor priest is overburdened with wife and child, his conscience troubled." Luther took issue with the legal prohibition of clerical marriage, arguing from Scripture that marriage is neither precluded nor required; rather, he was convinced that since scripture did not preclude marriage, evangelical freedom should supersede the strictures of canon law: "my advice is restore freedom to everybody and leave every man free to marry or not to marry." Astutely, Luther recognized that such a shift would require different church policy as well as the elimination of certain canon laws.[12]

Despite the huge ramifications of his actions for the status quo, Luther steadily worked on behalf of priests who were already living with spouses and children. Finding resources in Pauline literature to the effect that a bishop should be the husband of but one wife, Luther proclaimed that ministers should be "given liberty by a Christian council to marry to avoid temptation and sin." In moving prose Luther claimed that despite the condemnation of canon law, if "from the bottom of their hearts both are of a mind to live together in lawful wedded love, . . . the two are certainly married in the sight of God." His authority for offering this pronouncement was not his clerical office nor his professorial appointment but rather his simple claim to "the authority of a Christian to advise and help my neighbor against sins and temptations."[13]

Over time, Luther elaborated his defense of sexuality and marriage while following the basic method of experience brought to careful study of scripture. Increasingly, a theology of creation dominated his writing on sexuality and marriage. First, Luther learned from Genesis 1:27 (God created them male and female) to claim that each of us are and can only be exactly what God created us to be and moreover that we should honor God's delightful handiwork. One should not deride the other but

---

12. Luther, "To The Christian Nobility," 176. Cf. This comment from Luther's *Tabletalk*: "The stupid canon lawyers want to apply laws that were framed in other times and for other reasons. They say, 'Thus it is written in the book,' and they don't see that the times have changed and that former circumstances and laws have passed away." Martin Luther, "Marriage Laws must be Adapted to the Times (1539)," in *LW 54*, 349.

13.Luther, "To The Christian Nobility," 177.

honor their bodily distinctiveness. For Luther, the body in all its physical sense and wholeness should be seen "as a divine and good creation that is well-pleasing unto God himself."[14] Luther used this argument about the goodness of human bodily nature to encourage monks and nuns in leaving monastic vows for marriage as well as to undergird the general goodness of marriage as a civil estate intended for all people and the specific appropriateness of marriage for Christians.[15]

Second, drawing from Genesis 1:28 (Be fruitful and multiply), Luther claims that sexual desire is as natural as sleeping and drinking and moving the bowels; whenever one tries to resist this, "it remains irresistible nonetheless and goes its way through fornication, adultery, and secret sins, for this is a matter of nature and not of choice."[16] Writing on the sixth commandment, Luther commented that where "nature has its way, as God implanted it, it is not possible to remain chaste outside of marriage; for flesh and blood remain flesh and blood, and the natural inclinations and stimulations have their way without let or hindrance, as everyone's observation and experience testify."[17] Kristen Kvam notes that some early church fathers regarded sexual desire as clear evidence of the corruption of humanity: it was neither present in the original creation nor will it be in the coming Reign of God. In this context, Luther's affirmation of the sex drive and sexual relationship as a fundamental aspect of God's good creation mark a bold turn in his theology.[18]

Luther's strong doctrine of sin deeply mars this good creation, however. In the original state of creation, Luther could say of sexual intercourse "in Paradise that union would have taken place without any bashfulness, as an activity created and blessed by God. It would have been accompanied by a noble delight, such as there was at the time in eating and drinking. Now, alas, it is so hideous and frightful a pleasure

---

14. Luther, "The Estate of Marriage," 17.

15. For a remarkable and provocative contemporary exploration of the question of bodily experience in sexual ethics, written by a Lutheran woman, see Mary D. Pellauer, "The Moral Significance of Female Orgasm: Toward Sexual Ethics That Celebrates Women's Sexuality," *Journal of Feminist Studies in Religion* 9 (Spring/Fall 1993): 161-182.

16. Luther, "The Estate of Marriage," 17.

17. Luther, "The Large Catechism," in Tappert, ed. *The Book of Concord*, 393-394.

18. Kvam, "'Honoring God's Handiwork," 179-180.

that physicians compare it with epilepsy or falling sickness."[19] Sin distorts the original goodness of the body and thus humans neither regard God, other humans, nor the world with proper faith, trust, and love. Under the conditions of sin, Luther suggests that marriage is proper in order to bear children, to provide companionship, and as an "antidote against sin" by which he meant that by committing to one sexual partner, one's lust could be guided away from many sinful behaviors. On the basis of natural sexual desires, therefore, Luther not only opposed compulsory celibacy and supported marriage, he also defended marriage as a place where Christians can be sure that they are doing God's will. "They can therefore," Luther wrote, "also be certain that the estate of marriage and everything that goes with it in the way of conduct, works, and suffering is pleasing to God."[20]

It may be striking to see Luther speak of the lustful corruption of sexual desire in one breath and in the next praise all aspects of Christian conduct, works, and suffering in marriage. Luther firmly believed that through the gift of grace, forgiveness, and new life in Christ, one takes on a new righteousness. Though Luther spoke of this new righteousness as "alien", given by Christ as a cloak to cover human sinfulness, nonetheless under this cloak the original righteousness begins a restoration which finds completion in the coming Reign of God. The ordinary work of household duty, even the father changing dirty diapers, are properly good works--they do not achieve goodness in God's eyes but serve the neighbor. These simple works required of relationship "are pleasing to God who has so ordained them, and thereby graciously cares for us like a kind and loving mother."[21]

Lastly, Luther draws on Genesis 2: 22 (And God brought her to Adam) in order to show God's original intention that humans are not meant to live alone but to have someone with whom to share the joys and burdens of life. Marriage, therefore, is intended by God as an equal relationship of shared intimacy and commitment. Luther writes of Adam and Eve that whatever "the husband has, the wife has and possesses in its entirety. Their partnership involves not only their means but children, food, bed, and dwelling; their purposes, too, are the

19. Luther, "Lectures on Genesis 1-5," 119.
20. Luther, "Estate of Marriage," 38.
21. Ibid., 43.

same."[22] Though sin also corrupts this original equality, still Luther expects each person "to love and cherish the wife or husband whom God has given. For marital chastity it is above all things essential that husband and wife live together in love and harmony, cherishing each other wholeheartedly and with perfect fidelity."[23]

Thus, from a revisioning of a theology of creation, Luther comes full circle from his experience of Christians in distress over untenable sexual prescriptions to a reexamination of scripture to a new view of theology of sexuality and marriage. On the basis of these foundations, Luther--at his best--expressed an earthy and often colorful embrace of bodily life. Luther's proposal for revisioning prescriptive rules for sexual ethics combines the three levels of human experience which Gustafson elaborates: nature (biological and personal) sin, and covenant. Luther saw the importance of sexuality both in its biological and personal aspects. He took care to warn about the sinful temptations and harm which accompany sexuality. He affirmed the importance of marriage as a covenant which protects against temptations to sin while also offering a context for loving, cherishing, and serving one's nearest of neighbors, a spouse.

Luther's theological method and his fundamental theological ideas can be of great service to contemporary theological efforts. First, Luther's outrage at the suffering of people under unjust imposition of celibacy led him to a reexamination of scripture in order to assist those under distress. His worries about canon law and church structure developed out of pastoral concerns, and though he attended to them, he first attended to those unjustly burdened. Many people today, once hearing the witness of gay and lesbian Christians, would not doubt that the same sort of situation Luther confronted exists today. Gay and lesbian clergy and candidates for ministry are forced into options which cause untold suffering: work in the ministry and remain celibate, leave the ministry in order to have the companionship, joy, and physical intimacy a partnership affords, or, as in Luther's time, keep one's companion secretly while remaining in the priesthood.

As I show in previous chapters, the theological problem with this situation lies in the use of an ahistorical reading of the traditional "orders of creation" theology. The scriptural texts regarding creation

---

22. Luther, "Lectures on Genesis 1-5," 137.
23. Luther, "The Large Catechism," 394.

and sexuality are read as if they describe an "ideal form" of marriage, a pattern to be emulated exactly in all times and places. This ideal has developed from what is now called a "heterocentrist" perspective that suggests a single male-female pairing to be the only acceptable pairing for marriage. Therefore, because the church does not recognize nor bless the marriages of gay and lesbian Christians, if they are called to pastoral ministry they must accept celibacy or secrecy as the only alternatives.

While it does not take too much imagination to see parallels between compulsory celibacy today and in Luther's time, a contemporary parallel to Luther's turn to scripture in order to ground a revised theological and ethical position on marriage is not so easily discovered. The reasons for this problem have been discussed in detail many other places[24]; I will only mention what I find to be the relevant factors in the debate. First of all, regardless of one's subsequent interpretation, scriptural references to sex between men or between women contain no affirmation of same-sex marriage and sexuality. According to Biblical scholar Luke Timothy Johnson, scriptural texts that reject homosexuality (see especially: Lev. 18:22; Wis. 14:26; Rom. 1:26-27; 1 Cor. 6:9) do so because it is an example of *porneia*, "namely, that it is 'against nature,' an abomination offensive to God's created order." Johnson continues, "Leviticus and Paul considered homosexuality a vice because they assumed it was a deliberate choice that 'suppressed the truth about God'." To such a position, Johnson suggests, one must ask the question: "is that a fair assessment of

---

24. Among many works on these issues, see Robin Scroggs, *The New Testament and Homosexuality* (Minneapolis: Fortress, 1983); Patricia Beattie Jung and Ralph F. Smith, *Heterosexism: An Ethical Challenge* (Albany: State University of New York, 1993), 65-88; Bernadette J. Brooten, *Love Between Women: Early Christian Responses to Female Homoeroticism* (Chicago: University of Chicago Press, 1996); David McCarthy Matzko, "Homosexuality and the Practices of Marriage," *Modern Theology* 13:3 (July 1997):371-397; and ELCA, *Human Sexuality and The Christian Faith: A Study for the Church's Reflection* (Chicago: Division for Church in Society, 1991), 12-27. For articulate positions that fundamentally conflict with my own, see Richard B. Hays, *The Moral Vision of the New Testament* (San Francisco: Harpercollins, 1996); and Stanley J. Grenz, *Welcoming but Not Affirming: An Evangelical Response to Homosexuality* (Louisville: Westminster/John Knox, 1998).

homosexuality as we have come to understand it?" And Johnson's own answer speaks as well for me; he writes that

> many of us who have gay and lesbian friends and relatives have arrived with them at the opposite conclusion: For many persons the acceptance of their homosexuality *is* an acceptance of creation as it applies to them. It is emphatically *not* a vice that is chosen.[25]

Through the testimony of gay and lesbian Christians, the church is slowly learning that homosexuality is no more chosen that heterosexuality.

Furthermore, Genesis 1: 27-28 and Genesis 2:18-25 are central parts of a "heterocentrist" reading of the Scriptural witness to the issue of marriage. Harold Haas exemplifies this in the Lutheran tradition. His view of the "heterosexual order of creation" resulted from an effort to work against the feminist movement he felt was weakening traditional male-female gender roles. But the Genesis texts need not be used defensively to keep women or gays or any other threatening group in their place. If one returns to the texts with Luther, but with the experience of contemporary problems of exclusion and forced celibacy in mind, different conclusions are possible. After all, Luther was not a simple literalist with regard to Scripture. First of all, he distinguished between the Word, Jesus, and Scripture through which He is revealed. Luther was willing to exclude the books of James and Revelation because he did not feel they showed forth Christ. Luther thought one

> must deal openly with the Scriptures. From the very beginning the word has come to us in various ways. It is not enough simply to look and see whether this is God's word, whether God has said it; rather we must look and see to whom it has been spoken, whether it fits us. That makes all the difference between night and day.[26]

Further, Luther warned about following blindly the interpretations of Scripture made in previous generations. He wrote, regarding the interpretation of the early church fathers, that they "often speak as a

25. Johnson, *Scripture and Discernment*, 146.

26. Luther, "How Christians Should Regard Moses," in Lull, ed. *Martin Luther's Basic Theological Writings*, 145.

result of an emotion and of a particular mood which we do not have and cannot have, since we do not have similar situations."[27]

Therefore, as Luther turned to Scripture for texts which spoke to his day, so today also can the church look to Scripture for the foundational sources of God's good will. First, if we turn to Genesis 1:27 (God created them male and female), it would be possible to simply affirm that the text says what Luther says it does--we are each created to be what we are, no more. As Luther claimed that females and males should not belittle each other, so today we should not belittle those who are primarily oriented toward the opposite sex, those who are oriented to the same sex, nor those for whom strong attractions to both male and female are true. Such an affirmation does not displace the church's norm of marriage as a covenant of life-long fidelity between two people. Rather, Luther's proclamation that we should delight in God's handiwork gives a theological support to gay pride.

Of course these interpretive suggestions assume an argument that orientation is natural and God's intention in creation, an argument which cannot be made from Scriptural evidence. However, gay and lesbian people report over and over that for the vast majority "choice" was never an option.[28] They have from an early age understood themselves to be oriented as they are. Various sciences are searching for conclusive evidence to support this claim of "natural" or biological homosexuality and while the findings are not conclusive on the exact cause, clear evidence exists that by early childhood the orientation is set. I join Patricia Jung and Ralph Smith when they affirm

---

27. Luther, "Lectures on Genesis 1-5," 61.

28. Research is growing rapidly in this area, but for an overview of recent science on homosexuality see two chapters in Jeffery S. Siker, *Homosexuality in the Church: Both Sides of the Debate* (Louisville: Westminster/John Knox, 1994). Two evangelical authors, Stanton L. Jones and Don E. Workman, examine the findings in various studies from the perspective of their belief that homosexuality is morally wrong--see "Homosexuality: The Behavioral Sciences and the Church," 93-115; Chandler Burr sifts through the findings of scientific research from his perspective that homosexuality is morally neutral, like left-handedness--see "Homosexuality and Biology," 116-136. Also see the somewhat older work by Richard R. Troiden, *Gay and Lesbian Identity: A Sociological Analysis* (New York: General Hall, 1988).

> homosexuality as a part of God's original blessing for profoundly theological reasons. Given what we know about the centrality of sexuality to human personhood and about sexual orientation, to contend that homosexuality is an expression of the falleness of the world entails the conclusion that God is against homosexual people in the very fabric of their existence as human beings.[29]

Jung and Smith invoke Peter's words in Acts 10:15b to defend their position: "What God has made clean, you must not call profane."[30]

If God has created gay and lesbian people "clean," that is, good in their fundamental identity, then I must affirm as Luther did the goodness of human bodily nature. Further, on this basis, those ministers who are wrongly kept under a false vow of celibacy should consider themselves free to find a partner or not as they see fit in their life. Those who suffer under the secrecy of a committed relationship while serving a congregation should turn again to their consciences, consider themselves married in God's sight, and formalize their commitment with friends and clergy who will support them. The policies of the ELCA regarding sexual behavior are bankrupt and must fall sooner or later; it is up to faithful people, gay and straight, to speak out against such unjust and unloving treatment of our brothers and sisters in the faith. Not only within the church, but also in civil society, the created goodness of gay and lesbian people undergirds a struggle for marriage as legitimate option, a true and general civil estate intended for all people who wish it.

Second, drawing from Genesis 1:28 (Be fruitful and multiply), we could affirm with Luther that indeed, God has created a basic sexual desire that is as natural as sleeping and drinking and moving the bowels. This good passion, which serves to draw humans into relation with one another, needs to be held distinct from lust and sin

---

29. Jung and Ralph F. Smith, *Heterosexism*, 88.

29. Luke Timothy Johnson's entire book, *Scripture and Discernment*, is an extended reflection and application of the early church's struggle over the conversion of Gentiles. Johnson analyses the struggle to make this change as it is told by Luke in Acts 10-15. According to Johnson, the "Gentiles were 'by nature' unclean and were 'by practice' polluted by idolatry" (147). This argument allows Johnson to make some quite illuminating comparisons to the church today as it struggles with the inclusion of gay and lesbian people.

that, while central as well, are conflated in unhelpful ways for Luther. He came close to breaking away from this unfortunate western notion that sex equals sin; nevertheless, he only did so in his construal of the original creation and spoke quite traditionally about lust and sex even within such "a blessed and God-pleasing estate" as marriage.[31] However, knowledge about human physiology and psychology informs our common sense of healthy human experiences of sexuality; we know that passion brings joy and for some constitutes a way to know the wonder and love of God.

Yet, Luther's worry about lust and the dangers inherent in the sphere of sexuality are very important. Sex can be used to do the deepest violence. Women are attacked and raped with horrifying frequency in the United States; children are abused; marriages are broken through betrayal and adultery; pain and distrust are created when a person is simply used for another's sexual pleasure. Sin distorts the original goodness of the body and thus humans neither regard God, other humans, nor the world with proper faith, trust, and love. The strong influence of sin, according to Luther, impacts the interpretation of God's intention that marriage serve as an "antidote against sin". While the language is antiquated, the concept is not. A commitment to another provides a context in which the trust and intimacy inherent in sexuality are honored and built up, as well as a context which avoids many of the harms possible when lust drives one's choices.

Lastly, Luther drew from Genesis 2:22 (And God brought her to Adam) as a way to show that God is the author of marriage. This fact meant that in some form or another, in every culture, men and women form kinship systems which allow for doing of daily tasks and rasing of families. More central to my present task, however, is Luther's construal of what God intends marriage to be for Christians. Through the eyes of the Spirit, the Christian sees the tasks of committed relationship as opportunities to serve the neighbor in love.

The Lutheran use of a static view of marriage, sex differentiation, and even monogamy as unchangeable "orders of creation" does not honor the supple development of the doctrine of creation in Luther's able hands. Indeed, what I have laid out holds on to basic insights in Luther's the theology of creation. Can the church today adopt Luther's compassion for those pressed by natural urges, his embrace of

31. Luther, "The Large Catechism," 394.

embodiment, and yet break the mold of exclusively tying those to a static male/female dyadic argument such as Harold Haas' "heterosexual order of creation"?[32] The "orders", according to Lutheran theologian Carl Braaten, exist and change within the flux of history. This recognition helps to "break their linkage to an ethical conservatism that always finds it necessary to stand against every revolutionary development, thus denying the freedom of God to do a new thing or two in the world."[33] The experience of the church through hearing what God has done in so many gay and lesbian Christian lives calls forth such a new theological ethics of sexuality and marriage. And, in doing such a new theological ethics, the church would indeed find significant resources in Luther for supporting committed, covenantal relations between two persons, regardless of whether male or female.

U.S. Lutheranism

Although I raise important insights from other churches and studies over the last sixty years, I will focus my attention here on the study guide from the LCA *Sex, Marriage, and Family*.[34] I consider it the best constructive study U. S. Lutherans have officially adopted and it contains a perspective which informs much of what has already been written in this chapter. I draw out three main constructive positions useful for today (and each with parallels to my discussion of Luther above): a focus on revising the church's position to speak to a new situation; an affirmation of the goodness of sexuality; and a shift from biological interpretation of the "order of creation" to a more personal, covenantal one.

Sex, Marriage and the Family embodies a drive to reform the church's teaching on sexuality. At the outset of the study, the authors admit the confusion awaiting anyone trying to speak clearly on sexuality today. The context of the church's reflections today is so

---

32. Karen Bloomquist addresses these issues in a carefully argued paper, "How Adequate is the Category of 'Natural' for a Lutheran Sexual Ethic Today?," *Lutheran Theological Seminary Bulletin* (Winter 1993): 33-45.

33. Braaten, "God in Public Life," 235.

34. The study credits theologian Martin Heinecken, professor at the Philadelphia seminary, for writing the theological chapter from which I draw my primary materials in this section.

fundamentally different from generations past that some ethical prescriptions must be rethought. This has not been done by ignoring the past; first, the study suggests the necessity of "a serious attempt to get at the fundamental concepts and relationships that lay behind earlier judgements." Second, however, the church must consider that "aspects of human life can
change so radically that specific ethical judgements must sometimes be turned upside down if their essential meaning is to be preserved."[35] There comes a time when the letter of the law, written in another time and place, kills the spirit of the law which the search for justice and love intend.

Therefore, the theological argument aims to find a middle road between, on the one hand, those who would reject all that is new and unfamiliar and, on the other, those who would reject traditional arguments as unable to any longer provide helpful guidance in today's world. The study finds neither of these options offers integrity and thus aims to build a new position. While affirming that the church views itself bound to God's revelation in history, centering in the life, death, and resurrection of Christ, it does not follow that interpretations of the relevance of this revelation and its bearing on the world are "fixed principles." Instead, "restatement, therefore, is constantly necessary; misunderstandings need to be corrected; attempts at enlargement need to be made. Sometimes entirely new approaches have to be developed which, however, do not lose their continuity with the past."[36]

Such efforts at a new approach in sexual ethics found expression in the ALC, as well. Its 1980 statement, *Human Sexuality and Sexual Behavior*, followed years of innovative and critical "action research" at the University of Minnesota, a program that resulted in training for both lay and clergy. Such a research program, based in current social science perspectives, influenced the breath of sources drawn up in the process of writing the ALC statement. They explicitly drew on traditional sources such as the bible, theology, and church history. However, they also strongly drew on recent research in psychology and sociology, allowing them to write a much more positive section on homosexuality that Karl Schmidt's work the previous 1966 statement.

35. *Sex, Marriage, and Family*, ed. Tilberg, 18.
36. Ibid., 45.

A second main contribution from the predecessor church statements lies in their strong affirmation of the goodness of sexuality. Granted, the LCA study, *Sex, Marriage, and the Family*, affirms the goodness of sex, in the same breath it warns of the dangers. In its expression, sex "can both create and destroy at the deepest levels of human life and personality."[37] Yet sex and sin are by no means to be equated even though they often appear, the study admits, profoundly intermixed in human experience. The author hints that the covenantal language in Scripture shows the deeply spiritual possibility of sexual relationships: both God's commitment to God's chosen people and the most intimate sexual relations are referred to with the phrase "to know." The ALC statement, *Human Sexuality and Sexual Behavior*, also moved beyond a narrow view on this point: while sexual behavior is clearly God's design for continuing the human race, sex also serves in "enhancing joy and renewing the vows of love and marriage."[38]

The shift in focus from a natural and biological interpretation of marriage as an "order of creation" to a more relational, covenantal interpretation of marriage marks the last main contribution from the predecessor church studies. The idea of a covenant governing relationships leads to the affirmation in *Sex, Marriage and the Family* that marriage is a "structure of God's created order." Directly after this phrase, the study recognizes the danger of the language of "orders": "'God's created order' needs explanation, however, lest it be regarded as some kind of static order of the past into which all of human life is molded."[39] Creation is not finished "in the beginning" but is the constant activity of a dynamic and living God. The truth of this language about marriage as a structure of creation is the truth that humans were not created to live alone; in fact one cannot even become human save through relationships with others. Marriage represents, therefore, a basic structure of human community; a context in which "humanness" is nurtured.

The study centers this structure in "a life-long, covenanted union of one man and one woman, based on fidelity . . ." Further, Jesus' injunction regarding this bond in Matthew 19:3-9 refers to the basic

37. Ibid., 47.

37. *Human Sexuality and Sexual Behavior*, 1.

39. *Sex, Marriage, and Family*, ed. Tilberg, 18.

"conditions and possibilities of the human situation."[40] Yet form, while important, is not as important as the dynamics of interrelationships. The ALC moved in this direction, as well. Even in Karl Schmidt's writings in the 1960s, a strong emphasis on relationship balanced his strong biological claims about a "one flesh union" between husband and wife.

The structure of marriage, intended by God for humanity in general, does not constitute what is Christian. Indeed, there is not such a thing as "Christian marriage." For Lutherans, marriage is a civil estate which Christians affirm and fulfill out of particular motivations and therefore in particular ways. The Scriptural injunction that marriage be a "one-flesh union" found of Genesis 2:24 and echoed by Jesus in Matthew 19:5 looms large in interpretations of Christian marriage.

The authors of *Sex, Marriage, and the Family* admit that two avenues are possible for interpreting this traditional statement. The first, drawing from St. Paul in I Corinthians 6:15-20 and connecting "one flesh" with sexual intercourse, suggests that by its nature sex affects the participants ontologically. This view was developed by Harold Haas in the 1950s and Carl Braaten in the 1960s. The study appreciates the seriousness that this view gives to sex but finds no empirical justification for such a claim. It seems, rather, to serve polemical and political uses in defensive theological arguments. The study takes the second view, drawing from Ephesians 5:21-23 and connecting "one flesh" with the gift of one's whole being to another. Christ and his bride, the church, provide the direct biblical symbolism, while the covenantal tradition in Hebrew Scriptures provides a deeper background. On the basis of this position, the study suggests that the "essence of marriage is that two people voluntarily take each other and promise fidelity."[41] The church and state only witness and legally validate the marriage which has been entered into by the individuals themselves.

I began this chapter asking the question whether Lutherans can build a theological and ethical position on marriage and sexuality that both fully welcomes lesbian and gay Christians and upholds the fundamental bases of church teachings on marriage and sexuality. The LCA study *Sex, Marriage, and Family,* suggests the "homosexual should not be judged a 'sinner' because of his homosexuality, but because he is a

---

40. Ibid, 50.
41. Ibid., 52.

'sinner' in the same way that everyone else is, viz., because he is alienated from God, self, the neighbor, the world."[42] The study suggests that the essence of marriage is that two people voluntarily take each other and promise fidelity. Further, even with the study's affirmation of traditional marriage between one man and one woman as God's intention, *Sex, Marriage, and the Family* suggests other forms are also possible and beneficial to individuals and society. What these other forms are, the study leaves to the readers imagination. Given these suggestive positions, I ask: why, then, could a gay or lesbian couple not also voluntarily take each other and promise fidelity? Or, to bring the question up to date and sharpen it a bit, why, when gay and lesbian couples *do indeed* voluntarily take each other and promise fidelity, does the church not recognize and bless what is a marriage in the sight of God? It seems to me that the burden of proof is on the church to show why it should not support, encourage, and bless such covenantal unions as authentic embodiments of our best teaching on sexuality and marriage.

Such an affirmation does not in any way denigrate, as *Sex, Marriage and Family* makes clear, the church's support for the traditional pattern of male-female marriage. Rather, it simply means that marriage cannot be seen as exclusively the domain of traditionally male-female couples. Theologically, the exclusive reservation of marriage for male/female couples is neither justified nor truthful to contemporary experience: most fundamentally, marriage recognizes natural human needs, sexual and personal; the need for protections against abuse; and structures of commitment which foster trust and fidelity. Traditional Lutheran theological sources support these fundamental affirmations and in no way depend on male/female patterns for marriage.[43] The test of the church will be the ways it moves to reform ethical prescriptions, liturgical rubrics, and governing policies. These would need to follow an affirmation of the theological position for which I have argued in this chapter if the church is to be a serious and faithful partner in dialog with its lesbian and gay members, candidates for ministry, and pastors. In short, these would need to follow if the church is to fulfill its own rhetoric that "gay and lesbian people, as individuals created by God, are

---

42. Ibid., 63.
43. Jung and Smith make a similar argument in *Heterosexism*, 140-151.

welcome to participate fully in the life of congregations [of the ELCA]."[44]

42. ELCA, "The Ordination of Non-Celibate Gay and Lesbian Persons (1999), *Churchwide Assembly Action CA99.06.27.*

Conclusion

Theology and Social Change

At a recent professional meeting, I observed a senior Lutheran ethicist listening to discussions regarding strategies for moving churches toward more affirming positions on gay and lesbian members. After a presentation on a potential ethic for same-sex relationships which provoked a heated discussion, the senior ethicist, both straight and male, offered a simple and basic observation based on his own experience of changing views on the subject at hand. He said he had changed his mind after meeting and listening to gay and lesbian Christians. His experience with these particular people pressed him to move from regarding "them" as an "issue" to regarding "our" life together as unjustly exclusive and in need of revision.[1]

I too have had such an experience of interpersonal re-formation, an experience which led to the book now before you. I would venture to guess that if you have read through the book this far, you, the reader, have had such an experience as well. I wrote the book because, as Timothy Lull has said, "while theology alone will not change things, it will be hard for Lutherans to move forward without a better rationale for what we are doing and how we see this change in continuity with our heritage."[2] I have contributed to building such a "theological rationale" for change in the church. Yet, without also having some personal experience with gay and lesbian persons, I am not convinced

1. See his recent book that argues for change in the church's teaching on homosexuality. Paul Jersild, *Spirit Ethics: Scripture and the Moral Life* (Minneapolis: Fortress Press, 1999), esp. 129-148.

2. Lull, "Learning from the Reformers," 62.

that the arguments of a book alone can bring a new mind and heart. My arguments are certainly not cogent enough nor persuasive enough alone to convince people of good faith that their gay brothers and sisters share that faith, carry the image of God in themselves, and are created good. Therefore, opportunities must be found to tell stories.[3]

Current ELCA bishop Paul Wennes Egertson, whose eldest of four sons is gay, tells the story of he and his wife, Shirley, as they made the transition from condemnation to celebration. Their story--as they tell it today--is in response to the question, "What do you say after someone you love says, "I'm gay"? They share their story not because it is unique but because it is so typical of the way many parents and friends respond to the news that a loved one is gay.[4]

Bishop Egertson recounts the transition using the image of God's seven days of creation, with each day representing a new stage in transformation. The first day, upon hearing the news that their eldest son was gay, their first reaction was to deny it. They knew little about homosexuality but thought it was "obviously a distortion of nature prohibited by both Scripture and common sense." Yet, they knew a great deal about their son; an honors student at California Lutheran and a devout Christian, he planned to attend seminary and enter the ordained ministry of the Lutheran church. Their response was to think he was just going through a phase, that "when the right girl comes along he will resolve it."[5]

When things did not change and they could no longer deny it, the second stage took hold--they sought to explain it. Given their ignorance of research on homosexuality, they thought either he had chosen it or it was the result of bad parenting. After much reflection and conversation, neither seemed to be the case, and their journey of education began. They found that the social and natural sciences have a number of theories attempting to explain homosexuality but currently, no single cause is know. However, it is known that across cultures,

---

3. I note here the recent release of Pam Walton's "Call To Witness: A video documentary about the courageous struggle for gay and lesbian rights within the Lutheran Church," an hour-long exploration of the stories of gay and lesbian pastors in the ELCA.

4. Bishop Paul Wennes Egertson, "One Family's Story," in Walter Wink, ed. *Homosexuality and Christian Faith: Questions of Conscience for the Churches* (Minneapolis: Fortress Press, 1999).

5. Egertson, "One Family's Story," 24.

nations, races, and classes, a small but consistent number of people seem to be homosexual. Bishop Egertson notes that in their research, they learned that no one understands exactly what causes heterosexuality, either.

When they could not deny or explain it, the Egertson's sought to fix it. It turns out that their son had already tried this. Knowing from an early age that he was different, and that this difference was something unacceptable to God, he had prayed nightly that God would change him. When the Egertson's pursued psychological therapy, they found that most psychiatrists and psychologists had already changed from viewing homosexuality as an illness to viewing it as a natural part of one's identity--and therapy should therefore help one to accept it "before the socially imposed shame and the personal pain drive them to despair, drink, drugs, or death by suicide, all of which it does daily to numerous persons."[6]

Thus, the Egertson's faced the fourth "day" of their process: mourning. They could have dealt with the situation as a death of their son, saying to him that since he is homosexual, he is no longer a son to them. Though this is the path of some parents and even some congregations, the Egertson's took another path: they dealt with the situation as a death of their own misunderstandings, ignorance, and attitudes. They mourned the loss of a black and white view of sexual ethics (and the proof texts from the bible that back it up). And they mourned the loss of their hopes for ordinary happiness for their child--including his hoped-for entrance into the ordained ministry.

As they mourned these deaths, they saw that they were focussing less on themselves and more on the struggles their son faced. This turn moved them toward the fifth "day" of their journey, a journey that led them from initial denial to acceptance. At this point, their son had come to affirm his identity and they were able to realize that "*the biggest problem in being gay is not the gayness, but the reaction of heterosexuals to it*" [emphasis in the original].[7] They admitted that they could not change their son; they could, however, work to change the biases of those who, like themselves, did not understand what it is to be gay.

---

6. Ibid, 26.
7. Ibid, 28.

Today, the Egertson's have reached a sixth "day" in the creation of their view of homosexuality. They celebrate it! They show this is possible, but only with a particular view of what homosexuality is, and they describe four. First, homosexuality can be seen as a conscious choice, a rebellion against God, and thus would call for repentance rather than celebration. Second, it can be seen as an illness, like alcoholism, that should not be celebrated but solved through abstinence and therapy. Third, homosexuality can be viewed as a tragedy of nature, like a physical disability, and thus calling for compassionate assistance but not celebration. Finally, one can view homosexuality, as the Egertson's have come to do, as a variety in nature, a delightful surprise in God's wide and diverse creation. In this case, it is seen as analogous to left-handedness, something that not too many years ago was also seen as deviant and in need of punishment and correction. Now, however, left-handedness is seen as neutral or even, in the case of baseball, for instance, something highly desirable. Viewed in this way, homosexuality can be celebrated as a gift of God.

On the seventh day, Bishop Egertson wrote, having moved from condemnation and denial to acceptance and celebration of their gay son, they rested. So too, now, will I rest. This book of critical history and constructive retrieval will be worth the writing if it can in some way put theology into the service of social change, if it can in some way assist the church in its own seven day journey from condemnation and denial to acceptance and celebration.

Bibliography[1]

1997 ELCA Churchwide Assembly: A Brief Summary of Actions. Chicago: Department for Communications, Evangelical Lutheran Church in America, 1997.

"ALC and LCA precedents." *The Lutheran*, 16 March 1988, 23.

"Almen: ELCA is Visible, Vulnerable." *The Lutheran*, 1 June 1988, 24

Althaus, Paul. *The Ethics of Martin Luther.* Translated by Robert Schultz. Philadelphia: Fortress, 1972.

The American Lutheran Church. *Official Minutes of the Fourteenth Convention held in Blue Island, Illinois, October 4-11, 1956.* Columbus: The Wartburg Press, 1956.

The American Lutheran Church. *Reports and Actions of the Tenth Convention held in Minneapolis, Minnesota, October 1-7, 1980.* Arnold R. Mickelson, ed. Minneapolis: Office of the Secretary, The American Lutheran Church, 1980.

The American Lutheran Church. *Reports and Actions of the Ninth Convention held in Morehead, Minnesota, October 18-24, 1978.* Arnold R. Mickelson, ed. Minneapolis: Office of the Secretary, The American Lutheran Church, 1978.

1. References to writings by Martin Luther found in *Luther's Works, American Edition, 55 Volumes*. General Editors, Jaroslav Pelikan and Helmut T. Lehmann. St. Louis: Concordia Publishing House (1-30) and Philadelphia: Fortress Press (31-55), 1957-1967, will be referenced according to title and date of the writing by Luther, the translator, and the pages in the relevant volume of the above series, followed by the abbreviation *LW* and the number of the volume in which the writing is found.

The American Lutheran Church. *Reports and Actions of the Third Convention held in Minneapolis, Minnesota, October 19-25, 1966.* William Larsen, ed. Minneapolis: Office of the Secretary, The American Lutheran Church, 1966.

The American Lutheran Church. *Reports and Actions of the Second Convention held in Columbus, Ohio, October 21-27, 1964.* William Larsen, ed. Minneapolis: Office of the Secretary, The American Lutheran Church, 1964.

"Anglicans on homosexuality." In The Christian Century 115. August 12-19, 1998, 742-743.

Ariès, Philippe and André Béjin. *Western Sexuality: Practice and Precept in Past and Present Time.* Translated by Anthony Forster. New York: Basil Blackwell, 1985.

Atkinson, Clarissa. *The Oldest Vocation: Christian Motherhood in the Middle Ages.* Ithaca: Cornell, 1991.

"The Augsburg Confession." In *The Book of Concord*, Translated and Edited by Theodore G. Tappert, 23-96. Philadelphia: Fortress Press, 1959.

Bainton, Roland H. *Here I Stand: A Life of Martin Luther.* New York: Mentor Books, 1950.

Baum, Gregory. "Homosexuality and the Natural Law." *The Ecumenist* 1 (January-February 1994): 33-36.

Bellah, Robert, Richard Madsen, William M. Sullivan, Ann Swidler, and Steven M. Tipton. *Habits of the Heart: Individualism and Commitment in American Life.* Berkeley: University of California Press, 1985.

Billing, Einar. *Our Calling.* Translated by Conrad Bergendoff. Social Ethics Series, ed. Franklin Sherman, no. 1. Philadelphia: Fortress, 1964.

"Bishops: Gay Clergy Must Be Celibate." *The Lutheran*, 30 March 1988, 24.

"Bishops' 'Intervention' Questioned." *The Lutheran*, 11 May 1988, 26.

Blakely, Edward J. And Mary Gail Snyder. *Fortress America: Gated Communities in the United States.* Palo Alto: Brookings Institution, 1996.

Bloomquist, Karen. "How Adequate is the Category of 'Natural' for a Lutheran Sexual Ethic Today?" *Lutheran Theological Seminary Bulletin* (Winter 1993): 33-45.

Braaten, Carl E. *Eschatology and Ethics: Essays on the Theology and Ethics of the Kingdom of God.* Minneapolis: Augsburg Publishing House, 1974.

________. "God in Public Life: A Rehabilitation of the Lutheran Idea of the 'Orders of Creation'." In *Encounters With Luther, Vol. IV*, ed. Eric W. Gritsch, 232-250. Gettysburg: GAM Printing, 1990; Reprinted in *First Things* 1:8, December 1990:32-38.

________. "Reflections on the Lutheran Doctrine of the Law," 72-84. In *The Lutheran Quarterly* 18. February 1966.

________. "Sex, Marriage and the Clergy." *dialog* 18 (Summer 1979): 169-174.

Braaten, Carl E. And Robert Jenson, eds. *Union With Christ: The New Finnish Interpretation of Luther.* Grand Rapids: Eerdmans, 1998.

Brecht, Martin. *Martin Luther: Shaping and Defining the Reformation 1521-1532.* Translated by James L. Schaaf. Minneapolis: Fortress Press, 1990.

Brooten, Bernadette. *Love Between Women: Early Christian Responses to Female Homoeroticism.* Chicago: University of Chicago Press, 1996.

Bussert, Joy M. K. *Battered Women: From a Theology of Suffering to an Ethic of Empowerment.* New York: Lutheran Church in America, 1986.

Burtness, James H. "The New Morality: Some Biographical Comment." *dialog* 5 (Winter 1966): 10-17.

Cahill, Lisa Sowle. "Silencing of Nugent, Gramick sets a novel standard of orthodoxy." In *America* 181. August 14, 1999: 6-10.

"Case of Gay Elder goes before PCUSA court." In *The Christian Century* 115. January 21, 1988: 50-51.

The Christian and His Social Living. Minneapolis: Board for Christian Social Action, American Lutheran Church, 1960.

The Church and Human Sexuality: A Lutheran Perspective. Chicago: Division for Church in Society, Department of Studies of the Evangelical Lutheran Church in America, 1993.

"Church Council OKs Mission 90." *The Lutheran*, 24 May 1989, 21-23.

Crantz, F. Edward. *An Essay on the Development of Luther's Thought on Justice, Law, and Society.* Cambridge: Harvard, 1959.

"The Crucible of Kosovo: Top Religion Stories of 1999." In *The Christian Century* 117, January 5-12, 2000, 20-21.

"Defying Church Law." In *The Christian Century* 116. February 3-10, 1999:105-106.

Deleuze, Gilles. *Foucault.* Translated and Edited by Sean Hand. Minneapolis: University of Minnesota Press, 1986.

Division for Ministry. *Definitions and Guidelines for Discipline.* Chicago: Office of the Secretary of the ELCA, 1990; See also *1989 Church Wide Assembly Reports and Records, Vol. II,* 546-548.

________. *Vision and Expectations: Ordained Ministers in the Evangelical Lutheran Church in America.* Chicago: Office of the Secretary of the ELCA, 1990.

Dreyfus, Hubert L. and Paul Rabinow. *Michel Foucault: Beyond Structuralism and Hermeneutics, Second Edition.* Chicago: University of Chicago Press, 1983.

Ebeling, Gerhard. "The Necessity of the Doctrine of the Two Kingdoms." In *Word and Faith.* Translated by James W. Leitch. Philadelphia: Fortress, 1963.

Edwards, Mark U., Jr. *Printing, Propaganda, and Martin Luther.* Berkeley: University of California Press, 1994.

Egertson, Bishop Paul Wennes. "Our Family's Story," 24-30. In *Homosexuality and the Christian Faith: Questions of Conscience for the Churches.* Walter Wink, ed. Minneapolis: Fortress Press, 1999.

Elert, Werner and Paul Althaus. "The Ansbach Response," 189-192. In *Two Kingdoms and One World: A Sourcebook in Christian Social Ethics.* Karl Hertz, ed. Augsburg: Minneapolis, 1976.

Ellingsen, Mark. "Luther on Human Sexuality." *dialog* 32 (Winter 1993): 69-74.

Ellison, Marvin. *Erotic Justice: A Liberating Ethic of Sexuality.* Louisville: Westminster/John Knox, 1997.

Eribon, Didier. *Michel Foucault.* Translated by Betsy Wing. Cambridge, Massachusetts: Harvard University Press, 1991.

Evangelical Lutheran Church in America. *Candidacy Manual.* Chicago: Office of the Secretary of the ELCA, 1994.

________. "The Ordination of Non-Celibate Gay and Lesbian Persons." Churchwide Assembly Action CA99.06.27. In *1999 Churchwide Assembly Reports and Records, Vol. I and II.* Chicago: Office of the Secretary of the ELCA, 2000.
________. 1999 *Church Wide Assembly Pre-Assembly Report.* Chicago: Office of the Secretary of the ELCA, 1999.
________. *1993 Church Wide Assembly Reports and Records, Vol I.* Chicago: Office of the Secretary of the ELCA, 1994.
________. *1991 Church Wide Assembly Reports and Records, Vol. I.* Chicago: Office of the Secretary of the ELCA, 1992.
________. *1989 Church Wide Assembly Reports and Records, Vols I and II.* Chicago: Office of the Secretary of the ELCA, 1990.
________. *ELCA Constitutions, Bylaws and Continuing Resolutions.* 3d ed. Chicago: ELCA, 1993.
"ELCA to maintain stance on homosexuality." In The Christian Century 116. September 8-15, 1999, 843-844.
"The Extraordinary Candidacy Project: A Call To Action." Public brochure, Berkeley, CA, May 1994.
Fletcher, Joseph. *Situation Ethics: The New Morality.* Philadelphia: The Westminster Press, 1966.
Farley, Margaret. "The Role of Experience in Moral Discernment," 134-151. In *Christian Ethics: Problems and Prospects.* Lisa Sowle Cahill and James F. Childress, eds. Cleveland: The Pilgrim Press, 1996.
Forell, George W. *Faith Active in Love: An Investigation of the Principles Underlying Luther's Social Ethics.* Minneapolis: Augsburg, 1954.
________. "The Importance of Law for Sexual Ethics." *dialog* 32 (Winter 1993): 68-69.
________. "Luther and Christian Liberty." In *Encounters With Luther, Vol. IV*, ed. Eric W. Gritsch, 99-111. Gettysburg: GAM Printing, 1990.
________. "Luther's Conception of 'Natural Orders'." *The Lutheran Church Quarterly* 18 (April 1945): 160-177.
Foucault, Michel. *Discipline and Punish: The Birth of the Prison.* Translated by Alan Sheridan. New York: Vintage Books, 1979.
________. *The History of Sexuality: An Introduction.* Translated by Robert Hurley. New York: Vintage Books, 1990.

________. "The Archaeology of Knowledge." In *Foucault Live: Interviews 1966-84,* Translated by John Johnston and Edited by Sylvère Lotringer, 45-56. Columbia University, New York: Semiotext(e) Foreign Agents Series, 1989.

________. "Nietzsche, Genealogy, History." In *The Foucault Reader*, ed. Paul Rabinow, 76-100. (New York: Pantheon Books, 1984), 77.

________. "Polemics, Politics, and Problemizations: An Interview with Michel Foucault." Interview by Paul Rabinow (May 1984). *The Foucault Reader*, ed. Paul Rabinow, 381-390. New York: Pantheon Books, 1984.

________. "Politics and Ethics: An Interview." Interview by Paul Rabinow, Charles Taylor, Martin Jay, Richard Rorty, and Leo Lowenthal (Berkeley, April 1983). *The Foucault Reader*, ed. Paul Rabinow, 373-380. New York: Pantheon Books, 1984.

________. "Politics and Reason." In *Michel Foucault, Politics, Philosophy and Culture: Interviews and Other Writings 1977-1984*, ed. Lawrence D. Kritzman, 58-85. New York: Routledge, 1990.

________. "The Subject and Power." In Hubert L. Dreyfus and Paul Rabinow, *Michel Foucault: Beyond Structuralism and Hermeneutics, Second Edition*, 208-226. Chicago: University of Chicago Press, 1983.

________. "Questions of Method." In *The Foucault Effect: Studies in Governmentality*, ed. Graham Burchell, Colin Gordon, and Peter Miller, trans. Colin Gordon, 73-86. Chicago: The University of Chicago Press, 1991.

________. "Two Lectures." In *Power/Knowledge: Selected Interviews and Other Writings, 1972-1977*, ed. Colin Gordon and trans. Colin Gordon, Leo Marshall, John Mepham, and Kate Soper, 78-108. New York: Pantheon Books, 1980.

________. "What is Enlightenment." In *The Foucault Reader*, ed. Paul Rabinow, 32-50. New York: Pantheon Books, 1984.

Fuerst, Westley, John Reumann, Franklin Shermann, Robert Benne, Gilbert Meilaender, and Blanche Jenson. "A Symposium on the LCA's Study of Homosexuality." *dialog* 26 (Spring 1987): 142-148.

Gandal, Keith, Stephen Kotkin, and Paul Rabinow, eds. *History of the Present: A Newsletter* 1 (February 1985).

Graebner, Alan. "Birth Control and The Lutherans: The Missouri Synod as a Case Study." In *Women in American Religion*, ed. Janet Wilson James, 229-252. Philadelphia: University of Pennsylvania Press, 1980.

Grentz, Stanley J. *Welcoming, Not Affirming: An Evangelical Response to Homosexuality*. Louisville: Westminster/John Knox, 1998.

Gustafson, James M. *Ethics from a Theocentric Perspective, Vol. I: Theology and Ethics*. Chicago: University of Chicago Press, 1981.

________. "Introduction." In H. Richard Niebuhr, *The Responsible Self: An Essay in Christian Moral Philosophy*, 6-41. New York: Harper and Row, 1963.

________. *Protestant and Roman Catholic Ethics: Prospects for Rapprochement*. Chicago: University of Chicago Press, 1978.

________. "Nature, Sin, and Covenant: Three Bases for Sexual Ethics." In *Perspectives in Biology and Medicine* (Spring 1981): 483-497.

Gutting, Gary. *Michel Foucault's Archaeology of Scientific Reason*. Cambridge: Cambridge University Press, 1989.

Haas, Harold. "Christian Faith and Family Life." In *Christian Social Responsibility, Vol. III, Life in Community*, ed. Harold C. Letts, 148-185. Philadelphia: Muhlenberg Press, 1957.

Haile, H. G. "Algorithm and Epikeia: Martin Luther's Experience with the Law." *Soundings* 61 (Winter 1978): 500-514.

Harrison, Beverly Wildung. "The Power of Anger in the Work of Love," 3-21. In *Making the Connections: Essays in Feminist Social Ethics*. Carol S. Robb, ed. Boston: Beacon Press, 1985.

Hartman, Keith. *Congregations in Conflict: The Battle over Homosexuality*. New Brunswick, New Jersey: Rutgers University Press, 1996.

Hauerwas, Stanley. *The Peaceable Kingdom: A Primer in Christian Ethics*. Notre Dame: University of Notre Dame Press, 1983.

Hays, Richard B. *The Moral Vision of the New Testament*. San Francisco: Harpercollins, 1996.

Hinlicky, Paul R. "Luther against the Contempt of Women." *Lutheran Quarterly* 2 (Winter 1988): 515-530.

Holl, Karl. *The Reconstruction of Morality*. Edited by James Luther Adams and Walter F. Bense. Translated by Fred W. Meuser and Walter R. Wietzke. Minneapolis: Augsburg, 1979.

Human Sexuality: The Findings of the Action Research Project in Human Sexuality of the Division for Service and Mission in America. Minneapolis: The American Lutheran Church, 1978.

Human Sexuality, Working Draft: A Possible Social Statement of the Evangelical Lutheran Church In America with Accompanying Documents. Chicago: Division for Church in Society of the ELCA, 1994.

Human Sexuality and Sexual Behavior. Minneapolis: The American Lutheran Church, 1980.

"It's Official: What ELCA Asks of Clergy." *The Lutheran*, 28 November 1990, 23-24.

Jacobs, Charles M. "Introduction to 'A Brief Explanation'." In *Works of Martin Luther, The Philadelphia Edition,* Vol. 2, 351-353. Philadelphia: Muhlenberg, 1943.

Jersild, Paul. *Spirit Ethics: Scripture and the Moral Life*. Minneapolis: Fortress, 1999.

Johnson, Luke Timothy. *Scripture and Discernment: Decision Making in the Church*. Nashville: Abingdon Press, 1996.

Jordan, Mark D. *The Invention of Sodomy in Christian Theology*. Chicago: University of Chicago Press, 1997.

Jung, Patricia Beattie and Ralph F. Smith. *Heterosexism: An Ethical Challenge*. Albany: The State University of New York Press, 1993.

Klein, Christa R. with Christian D. von Dehsen. *Politics and Policy: The Genesis and Theology of Social Statements in the Lutheran Church in America*. Minneapolis: Fortress Press, 1989.

Kvam, Kristin. "Honoring God's Handiwork: Challenges of Luther's Doctrine of Creation," 173-186. In *Reforming the Church . . .Gift and Task: Essays from a Free Conference*. Charles P. Lutz, ed. Minneapolis: Kirk House Publishing, 1995 .

Lattin, Don. "Americans Search For New Sex Ethic." *The San Francisco Chronicle*, 29 November 1994, 1, 6-7 (A).

Lazareth, William H. "ELCA Lutherans and Luther on Heterosexual Marriage." *Lutheran Quarterly* 8 (Autumn 1994): 235-268.

________. "Luther on Sex, Marriage, and Family." In *Crisis in Marriage*, eds. George W. Forell and William H. Lazareth, 58-64. Philadelphia: Fortress Press, 1978.

________. *Luther on the Christian Home: An Application of the Social Ethics of the Reformation.* Philadelphia: Muhlenberg, 1960.

________. "Orders." In *The Westminster Dictionary of Christian Ethics*, eds. James F. Childress and John Macquarrie, 441. Philadelphia: The Westminster Press, 1986.

Lazareth, William H., ed. *The Left Hand Of God: Essays on Discipleship and Patriotism.* Philadelphia: Fortress Press, 1976.

Lenski, Gerhard E. *Marriage in the Lutheran Church: A Historical Investigation.* Columbus, Ohio: The Lutheran Book Concern, 1936.

Levine, Donald N. "Rationality and Freedom: Weber and Beyond." *Sociological Inquiry* 51 (1981):5-26.

Longino, Helen E. *Science as Social Knowledge: Values and Objectivity in Scientific Inquiry.* Princeton: Princeton University Press, 1990.

Lull, Timothy F. "Introduction to Part I: The Task of Theology." In *Martin Luther's Basic Theological Writings*, ed. Timothy F. Lull, 7-12. Minneapolis: Fortress, 1989.

________. "LCA: A Church Called Lutheran." *The Lutheran,* December 1987, 12-14.

________. "Learning Reform from the Reformers." In *A Reforming Church . . . Gift and Task: Essays from a Free Conference*, 60-70. Charles P. Lutz, ed. Minneapolis: Kirk House Publishing, 1995.

________. "The (Normative) Sexual Hole." *dialog* 32 (Winter 1993): 65-68.

________. "Public and Private, Strong and Weak." *World and World* 10 (Spring 1990): 140-146.

Luther, Martin. "The Babylonian Captivity of the Church (1520)." Translated by A.T.W. Steinhäuser. Revised by Frederick C. Ahrens and Abdel Ross Wentz. 3-126. *LW* 36.

________. "A Brief Explanation of the Ten Commandments, The Creed, and The Lord's Prayer (1520)." Translated by Charles M. Jacobs, 354 -384. *PE* 2.

________. "Description of Luther's Tower Experience (1532)." Translated by Theodore G. Tappert, 193-194. *LW 54.*
________. "The Estate of Marriage (1522)." Translated by Walther I. Brandt, 12-40. *LW* 45.
________. "Examples of the Faulty Proofs of the Papists." Translated by Theodore G. Tappert, 323-324. *LW* 54.
________. "The Exposition of Psalm 127, For The Christians at Riga in Livonia." Translated by Walter I. Brandt, 311-337. *LW* 45.
________. "The Freedom of a Christian (1520)." Translated by Harold Grimm. Revised by Harold Grimm, 333-377. *LW* 31.
________. "How Christians Should Regard Moses." In *Martin Luther's Basic Theological Writings*, ed. Timothy F. Lull, 135-148. Minneapolis: Fortress, 1989.
________. "The Large Catechism." In *The Book of Concord: The Confessions of the Evangelical Lutheran Church*, trans. and eds. Theodore G. Tappert, et. al., 357-461. Philadelphia: Fortress Press, 1959.
________. "Lectures on Galatians 5-6 (1535)." Translated by Jaroslav Pelikan. 1-149. *LW* 27.
________. "Lectures on Genesis 1-5 (1535-1545)." Translated by George V. Schick. *LW* 1.
________. "Lectures on Genesis 15-20 (1535-1545)." Translated by George V. Schick. *LW* 3.
________. "Lectures on Genesis, 21-25 (1535-1545)." Translated by George V. Schick. *LW* 4.
________. "Letter To Three Nuns." Translated and edited by Theodore G. Tappert. In *Luther: Letters of Spiritual Counsel, The Library of Christian Classics*, 18. Edited by J. Baillie, J.T. McNeill, and H.P. Van Dusen. Philadelphia: The Westminster Press, 1955.
________. *Luther's Correspondence and Other Contemporary Letters*, Vol. 1, Translated and Edited by Preserved Smith and Charles Jacobs. Philadelphia: Lutheran Publication Society, 1913.
________. "Marriage Laws Must be Adapted to the Times (1539)." Translated by Theodore G. Tappert, 349. *LW* 54.
________. "The Ninety-Five Theses (1517)." In *Martin Luther's Basic Theological Writings*, Edited by Timothy F. Lull, 21-29. Minneapolis: Fortress, 1989.

______. "On Marriage Matters (1520)." Translated by Robert C. Schultz, 265-320. *LW* 46.

________. "Sermon at Marriage of Sigismund Von Lindenau (1545)." Translated and edited by John W. Doberstein, 357-367. *LW* 51.

________. "Sermons on the First Epistle of St. Peter (1523)," Translated by Martin H. Bertram, 2-145. *LW* 30.

________. "The Sermon on the Mount (1532)." Translated by Jaroslav Pelikan, 1-294.. *LW* 21.

________. "To The Christian Nobility of the German Nation Concerning the Reform of the Christian Estate (1520)." Translated by Charles M. Jacobs. Revised James Atkinson, 115-217. *LW* 44.

________. "Treatise on Good Works (1520)." Translated by W.A. Lambert. Revised by James Atkinson, 15-114. *LW* 44.

"Lutheran Headlines of '89." *The Lutheran*, 3 January 1990, 24.

Lutz, Charles P. *Public Voice: Social Policy Development in The American Lutheran Church, 1960-1987.* Minneapolis: Office of Church in Society, The American Lutheran Church, 1987.

________. "For the Battle-Weary: New Hope." In *A Reforming Church . . . Gift and Task: Essays from a Free Conference*, 10-13. Charles P. Lutz, ed. Minneapolis: Kirk House Publishing, 1995.

Lyles, Jean Caffey. "Discipline Policy: Too Legalistic?" *The Lutheran*, 20 December 1989, 22-23.

________. "Panel Suspends 2 S.F. Congregations." *The Lutheran*, 8 August 1990, 29.

________. "Western Bishops Back Action on Gays." *The Lutheran*, 16 March 1988, 23-24.

"Marriage and Divorce, Report of the Committee on Moral and Social Welfare." In *The United Lutheran Church In America, Minutes of the Seventh Biennial Convention, Milwaukee, WI, October 7-14, 1930,* 103-112. Philadelphia: The ULCA Publication House, 1930.

"Marriage and Family Statement, Report of the Board of Social Ministry." In *The Lutheran Church In America, Minutes of the Second Biennial Convention, Pittsburgh, Pennsylvania, July 2-9, 1964*, 494-496. Philadelphia: The LCA Board of Publication, 1964.

"Marriage and Family Life, Report of the Board of Social Missions." In *The United Lutheran Church In America, Minutes of the Twentieth Biennial Convention, Milwaukee, WI, October 10-17, 1956*, 1133-1146. Philadelphia: The ULCA Publication House, 1956.

Matzko, David McCarthy. "Homosexuality and the Practices of Marriage," Modern Theology 13 (July 1997):371-397.

McNeill, John T. "Natural Law in the Thought of Luther." *Church History* 10 (1941): 211-227.

A Message on Sexuality: Some Common Convictions. Chicago: Department of Studies, Division of Church in Society, Evangelical Lutheran Church in America, 1996.

Nelson, E. Clifford, ed. *The Lutherans in North America.* 2nd ed. Philadelphia: Fortress Press, 1980.

Nelson, James B. *Embodiment: An Approach to Sexuality and Christian Theology.* Minneapolis: Augsburg, 1978.

Niebanck, Richard J. "LCA: Church in the World." *The Lutheran*, December 1987, 25-27.

Niebuhr, H. Richard. *The Responsible Self: An Essay in Christian Moral Philosophy.* New York: Harper and Row, 1963.

Noelle-Neumann, Elisabeth. *The Spiral of Silence: Public Opinion--Our Social Skin.* 2d ed. Chicago: University of Chicago Press, 1993.

O'Donovan, Oliver. *The Desire of the Nations: Rediscovering the Roots of Political Theology.* Cambridge: Cambridge University Press, 1996.

Oberman, Hieko. *Luther: Man Between God and The Devil.* Translated by Eileen Walliser-Schwarzbart. New York: Doubleday, 1989.

Ozment, Steven. *The Age of Reform, 1250-1550: An Intellectual and Religious History of Late Medieval and Reformation Europe.* New Haven: Yale, 1980.

________. *Protestants: The Birth of a Revolution.* New York: Doubleday, 1992.

________. *When Fathers Ruled: Family Life in Reformation Europe.* Cambridge: Harvard, 1983.

Pellauer, Mary D. "The Moral Significance of Female Orgasm: Toward Sexual Ethics That Celebrates Women's Sexuality."

Journal of Feminist Studies in Religion 9 (Spring/Fall 1993): 161-182.

"Priest and Nun barred from ministry to gays." *The Christian Century* 116 (July 28-August 4, 1999):738.

Primmer, Margaret. "Letter to the Editor." *The Lutheran*, 20 April 1988, 48.

Rabinow, Paul. *French Modern: Norms and Forms of the Social Environment*. Cambridge, Massachusetts: The MIT Press, 1989.

________. "Representations are Social Facts: Modernity and Post-Modernity in Anthropology." In *Essays on the Anthropology of Reason*, 28-58. Princeton: Princeton University Press, 1996.

Rasmussen, Larry L. *Moral Fragments and Moral Community: A Proposal for Church in Society*. Minneapolis: Fortress, 1993.

Reuss, Carl F. "Courtship and Marriage." *The Lutheran Herald*, 7 April 1959, 6-7.

________. "Introduction." In *Sexual Integrity in Modern Society*, 2. Minneapolis: Commission on Research and Social Action, The American Lutheran Church, 1966.

Scharen, Christian Batalden. "Subject to Disciple: Authority, Sexuality, and the Production of Candidates for Ordained Ministry." In *Journal of the American Academy of Religion* 66 (Summer 1998): 89-120.

Scharffenorth, Gerta. *Becoming Friends in Christ: The Relationship Between Man and Woman as Seen by Luther*. Geneva: Lutheran World Federation, 1983.

Scroggs, Robin. *The New Testament and Homosexuality*. Minneapolis: Fortress, 1983.

Siker, Jeffery S., ed. *Homosexuality in the Church: Both Sides of the Debate*. Louisville: Westminster/John Knox Press, 1994.

Sittler, Joseph. "The Structure of Christian Ethics." In *Christian Social Responsibility, Vol. III, Life in Community*, ed. Harold C. Letts, 3-39. Philadelphia: Muhlenberg Press, 1957.

Stackhouse, Max. *Covenant and Commitments: Faith, Family, and Economic Life*. Louisville: Westminster/John Knox, 1997.

Stortz, Martha E. "Human Sexuality and the Christian Faith." *dialog* 32 (Winter 1993): 62-65.

Stout, Jeffery. *Ethics After Babel: The Language of Morals and Their Discontents.* Boston: Beacon Press, 1988.

A Study of Issues Concerning Homosexuality: Report of the Advisory Committee of Issues Related to Homosexuality. New York: Division for Mission in North America, Lutheran Church in America, 1986.

Swidler, Ann. "The Concept of Rationality in the Work of Max Weber." *Sociological Inquiry* 43 (1973): 35-42.

Szakolczai, Arpád. *Max Weber and Michel Foucault: Parallel Life-Works.* New York: Routledge Press, 1998.

"Text of Bishops' Statement." *The Lutheran*, 11 April 1990, 24.

Thielicke, Helmut. *The Ethics of Sex.* Translated by John W. Doberstein. New York: Harper and Row, 1964.

________. Theological Ethics, Vol. 1: Foundations. Edited by William H. Lazareth. Translated by John W. Doberstein. Philadelphia: Fortress, 1966.

Tilberg, Cedric, ed. *Sex, Marriage, and Family: A Contemporary Christian Perspective.* New York: The Lutheran Church in America, Division for Mission in North America, 1970.

"Top Stories of the Year." *The Lutheran*, 4 January 1989, 22-23.

Trelstad, Marit and Christian Scharen-Batalden. "Remembering RE-Imagining." *dialog* 33 (Summer 1994): 230-2.

Trexler, Edgar R. *Anatomy of a Merger: People, Dynamics, and Decisions that Shaped the ELCA.* Minneapolis: Augsburg, 1991.

________. "Bishops: Gay Ordinations Threaten Unity." *The Lutheran*, 11 April 1990, 24.

________. "CNLC Satisfies Most LCA Merger Issues." *The Lutheran*, July 1986, 18-19.

________. "The Issue of Ordaining Gays." *The Lutheran*, 16 March 1988, 50.

Troeltsch, Ernst. *The Social Teachings of The Christian Churches, Vol. I and II.* Translated by Olive Wyon. New York: Macmillian, 1931.

Troiden, Richard R. *Gay and Lesbian Identity: A Sociological Analysis.* New York: General Hall, 1988.

"Two Gays Ruled Out as Candidates." *The Lutheran*, 11 May 1988, 27.

The United Lutheran Church In America, Minutes of the Sixteenth Biennial Convention, Philadelphia, Pa., October 6-14, 1948. Philadelphia: The ULCA Publication House, 1948.

The United Lutheran Church In America, Minutes of the Twentieth Biennial Convention, Harrisburg, Pa., October 10-17, 1956. Philadelphia: The ULCA Publication House, 1956.

"UCC appoints minister to address gay issues." *The Christian Century* 114(April 9, 1997):359-360.

Weber, Max. "Bureaucracy." In *From Max Weber: Essays in Sociology*, eds. and trans. Hans H. Gerth and C. Wright Mills, 196-244. New York: Oxford University Press, 1946.

________. *The Protestant Ethic and the Spirit of Capitalism: The Relationships between Religion and the Economic and Social Life in Modern Culture.* Translated by Talcott Parsons. New York: Charles Scribner's Sons, 1958.

________. "The Social Psychology of the World Religions." In *From Max Weber: Essays in Sociology*, eds. and trans. Hans H. Gerth and C. Wright Mills, 267-301. New York: Oxford University Press, 1946.

Wentz, Abdel Ross. *A Basic History of Lutheranism in America.* Philadelphia: Fortress Press, 1955.

"Why Not Quiz All the Candidates?" *The Lutheran*, 11 May 1988, 27.

Wingren, Gustaf. *Luther on Vocation.* Translated by Carl C. Rasmussen. Philadelphia: Muhlenberg, 1957.

Witte, John Jr. *From Sacrament to Contract: Marriage, Religion, and Law in the Western Tradition.* Louisville: Westminster/John Knox, 1997.

Index

About the Author

Christian Batalden Scharen is currently a doctoral candidate in social ethics in the Graduate Division of Religion, Emory University. He is writing a dissertation in the area of liturgy and ethics titled *Public Worship and Public Work: Culture and Commitment in Local Congregational Life*. He has published articles in various journals on the subjects of sexuality and the church as well as liturgy and ethics.